PowerShell Troubleshooting Guide

Techniques, strategies and solutions across scripting, automation, remoting, and system administration

Steeve Lee

Copyright © 2024 by GitforGits

All rights reserved. This book is protected under copyright laws and no part of it may be reproduced or transmitted in any form or by any means, electronic or mechanical, including photocopying, recording, or by any information storage and retrieval system, without the prior written permission of the publisher. Any unauthorized reproduction, distribution, or transmission of this work may result in civil and criminal penalties and will be dealt with in the respective jurisdiction at anywhere in India, in accordance with the applicable copyright laws.

Published by: GitforGits
Publisher: Sonal Dhandre
www.gitforgits.com
support@gitforgits.com

Printed in India

First Printing: October 2023

ISBN: 9788119177271

Cover Design by: Kitten Publishing

For permission to use material from this book, please contact GitforGits at support@gitforgits.com.

Prologue

One of the most powerful entities that can be found in the enormous universe of computer languages and technologies is called PowerShell. To the uninformed, PowerShell may appear to be just another scripting language, but for those that dig deeper, it reveals itself to be a potent nexus between coding and systems administration. This is more than a tool; it's a force with the ability to weave automation magic in the heart of the Windows environment. You have found the "PowerShell Troubleshooting Guide," a map that will lead you to the hidden gems of this dynamic shell and help you find its optimal use.

Today's world is defined by technology and, more significantly, the efficiency with which it runs. Every millisecond saved, every process automated, and every error avoided results in considerable productivity benefits. In this respect, PowerShell is superior, providing administrators and developers with opportunities to automate, optimize, and innovate. The learning curve for PowerShell is steep, but the payoff is worth it in the end. The skill requires more than a head for numbers; it requires a mindset that is optimized for solving problems and becoming an expert user.

This book is an expedition, a precisely plotted route meant for both the novice entering the world of automation and the seasoned professional looking to sharpen their skills. You won't just learn about PowerShell's commands and syntax on its pages; you'll be immersed in a narrative that brings to life the very soul of this technology. We'll go on this trip together, beginning with the fundamentals and progressing through its complicated constructions to the pinnacle - where you may claim genuine mastery over PowerShell. Every chapter in this book is its own narrative. We decipher the mysteries of debugging, the art of creating efficient loops, the subtleties of error handling, and the complexities of remote network management. But this isn't just an informational monologue. It's a hands-on adventure. You will be invited to engage, code, experiment, and, most importantly, learn from real-world circumstances throughout this book. By the conclusion, you'll have not only knowledge but also experience, which is vital in the ever-changing world of technology.

PowerShell is more than just a bunch of code displayed on a screen. It's a symphony of logic, imagination, and possibility. While it is inherently linked to the Windows environment, its capabilities extend beyond, bridging gaps and making the complicated web of jobs that administrators and developers deal with on a daily basis smooth. Remote administration, system updates, event logs, and file transfers aren't just duties to be completed; they're difficulties to be conquered. This book will provide you with the plan, strategy, and skills to do just that. You'll learn not just the 'how' but also the 'why' in the pages that follow. Why is a specific function important? Why is one-way superior to another? Why should someone use PowerShell for automation and system management? These are some of the questions we'll look into to ensure that your understanding is comprehensive, deep, and long-lasting.

As you turn the pages, keep in mind that this isn't just a book; it's an experience. Whether you're a beginner just getting started with PowerShell or a seasoned pro wishing to enhance your skills, this journey will change your life. Let us go out on this journey, digging into the depths of PowerShell, defying traditions, pushing boundaries, and emerge as true automation maestros. Welcome to the "PowerShell Troubleshooting Guide" world. It is time to embark on this path of discovery.

Content

Preface xx

CHAPTER 1: INTRODUCTION TO POWERSHELL TROUBLESHOOTING 1

  Introduction 2

    Current State of PowerShell 2

    PowerShell Influence 3

    Challenges and Issues 3

  Setting up PowerShell on Windows 5

    Option #1: Direct Download from GitHub 6

    Option #2: Using Package Manager 7

    Option #3: Using PowerShell Deployment Toolkit 7

  Update PowerShell Core 8

    Option #1: Via GitHub 8

    Option #2: Via Package Manager 9

    Option #3: Using MSI 9

    Option #4: Using PowerShell Script 9

  PowerShell ISE 10

    Installing ISE via Windows Features 10

    Launching ISE 10

    Understanding ISE Interface 11

    Basic Customizations 11

    Debugging Features 12

    Modules and Add-ons 12

    ISE Profiles 13

    Working with Remote Sessions 13

  Navigate PowerShell ISE 13

    Menu Bar and Toolbar 13

    Keyboard Shortcuts 13

    Tab Expansion 14

Snippets 14
Context Menu 14
Variable Explorer 14
Command Add-on 14
Output Pane Customizations 14
Error List and Output List 14
Script Tabs 15
Context Highlighting 15
Find and Replace 15
Debugging Pane 15
Remote Tab 15

Essential PowerShell Commands 15
Get-Command 16
Get-Help 16
Get-Process 17
Get-Service 17
Set-ExecutionPolicy 17
Import-Module 18
New-Item 18
Remove-Item 19
Test-Connection 19
ConvertTo-Json 19

PowerShell in Cloud 20
PowerShell and Microsoft Azure 20
AWS Tools for PowerShell 20
Google Cloud PowerShell 20
Multi-Cloud Management 21
Cloud Automation and Scripting 21
Infrastructure as Code (IaC) 21
Security and Compliance 21
Monitoring and Logging 21

    Cost Management 21
  Summary 22
CHAPTER 2: UNDERSTANDING POWERSHELL COMMAND-LINE TOOLS **23**
  Command-Line Tools 24
  File Operations 25
    Get-ChildItem 25
    New-Item 25
    Set-Content and Add-Content 25
    Import-Csv and Export-Csv 25
    Remove-Item 26
    Get-FileHash 26
    Compress-Archive and Expand-Archive 26
    File Attributes with Get-Item and Set-ItemProperty 27
  Network Operations 27
    Test-Connection 27
    Test-NetConnection 27
    Get-NetIPAddress 27
    New-NetIPAddress and Remove-NetIPAddress 27
    Resolve-DnsName 28
    Get-NetRoute 28
    Get-NetTCPConnection and Get-NetUDPEndpoint 28
    Invoke-WebRequest and Invoke-RestMethod 28
    Get-NetFirewallRule and Set-NetFirewallRule 28
  Advanced Networking Functionalities 29
    New-NetSwitchTeam 29
    Set-DnsClientServerAddress 29
    Get-NetAdapterBinding 29
    Disable-NetAdapterBinding and Enable-NetAdapterBinding 29
    Get-NetNeighbor 29
    Get-NetTransportFilter and New-NetTransportFilter 30
    Get-NetTCPSetting and Set-NetTCPSetting 30

  Test-Connection with -MtuSize and -Ttl 30

  Invoke-Command with -Session 30

System Monitoring 30

  Get-Process 31

  Get-Service 31

  Get-EventLog 31

  Get-Counter 31

  Get-WmiObject 32

  Test-Connection for Continuous Ping 32

  Get-HotFix 32

  Measure-Command 32

  Get-Disk 33

  Get-NetAdapterStatistics 33

Text Manipulation 33

  Get-Content 33

  Set-Content 34

  Add-Content 34

  Out-File 34

  Select-String 34

  Replace Operator 35

  -split and -join Operators 35

  ConvertTo-Json and ConvertFrom-Json 35

  Format-Table and Format-List 35

  Sort-Object 36

Popular Flags and Parameters 36

  -Verbose 36

  -Force 36

  -Recurse 36

  -WhatIf 37

  -Credential 37

  -Filter 37

    -OutputFormat 37
    -Property 37
    -AsJob 38
    -Include and -Exclude 38
    -ErrorAction 38
Inbuilt Alias and Shortcuts 38
    Understanding Aliases 38
Summary 41

CHAPTER 3: WORKING WITH POWERSHELL ISE 43

PowerShell ISE Overview 44
ISE Interface and Components 45
ISE Customization 47
    Visual Elements 47
    Layout Customization 47
    Tabs and Files 47
    Custom Profiles and Functions 47
    Adding Custom Menu Items 48
    Debug Toolbar 48
    Creating Custom Key Bindings 48
ISE for Performance and Productivity 48
    "Layering" Approach 48
    Iterative, Shared and Team Customization 49
Script Debugging 50
    Debugging Environment in ISE 50
    Setting Breakpoints 50
    Stepping through Code 51
    Observing Variables 51
    Using Console Pane 51
    Advanced Breakpoints 51
    Script Output and Logs 52
PowerShell ISE Add-Ons 52

Your First Add-On 52
Advanced Customizations 53
Integrating External Tools 54
PowerShell ISE Object Model 55
Managing Files 55
Managing Tabs 55
Manipulating Options 56
Session Management 56
Additional Utilities 57
Integrate Git with PowerShell 57
Initial Setup 57
Git Add-Ons 58
Using Git 59
Custom GUI Extensions 59
Creating WPF Panel 60
Embedding WPF Panel into ISE 61
Code Refactoring 61
Importance 62
Sample Program: Refactoring Code in ISE 62
Summary 64
CHAPTER 4: POWERSHELL MODULES 66
Overview 67
Modules in PowerShell 67
Types of Modules 67
Install Complex Modules 69
From PowerShell Gallery 69
Manual Installation 70
Resolving Dependencies 70
Debugging Installations 71
Module Management 71
Module Inventory 71

Version Management 72
Module Dependencies 72
Updates 72
Uninstallation and Cleanup 72
Create Custom Cmdlets 73
Development Environment 73
Compiling and Testing 74
Parameters 74
Validation and Error Handling 74
Pipelining 75
Advanced Custom Cmdlet 76
Perform Error Handling 80
Using WriteError Method 80
Implementing Try-Catch Blocks 80
Summary 81

CHAPTER 5: SCRIPTING IN POWERSHELL 83
PowerShell Scripting Overview 84
Advantages of PowerShell Scripting 84
PowerShell Variables 85
Data Types 86
String Manipulation 86
Array and Hash Tables 86
Accessing Variables 86
Using Variables in Scripts 87
Scope of Variables 87
Special Variables 88
Data Types in Practice 88
Using Basic Data Types 88
Using Collections 89
Using Type Conversion and Casting 89
Using Type Constraints and Validation 89

Using Nullable Types 90
Dynamic Type Checking 90
Type Literals 90
The GetType() Method 90
Enumerations 90
Here-Strings 91
Custom Classes 91
Tuples and Custom Value Types 91
Record Types 92

Introduction to Conditional Statements 92
if, elseif, and else Statements 92
switch Statement 93
Wildcards and Regular Expressions 93
Ternary Operator 94
Nested Conditions 94
Where-Object Cmdlet 94
Conditional Execution with && and || 95
Exit Codes and $? 95
Sample Program: Using Conditional Statement 95

Understanding Loops and Iteration 98
Using for Loops for Scheduled Maintenance Checks 98
Utilizing foreach Loop for Array Iteration 98
Implementing while Loop for Conditional Repetition 99
Employing do-while and do-until for Postcondition Loops 99
Pipeline Iteration with ForEach-Object 99
Breaking and Continuing Loops 100

Diving into Functions and Parameters 101
Simplifying Code Blocks 101
Cmdlet Binding and Parameters 102
Pipeline Support in Functions 104

Dealing with Errors 104

Terminating vs. Non-terminating Errors 105
Try-Catch-Finally 105
$ErrorActionPreference 106
Custom Error Objects 106
Script Execution Policies 107
Types of Execution Policies 107
Setting Execution Policies 107
Viewing Execution Policies 108
Summary 109

CHAPTER 6: UNDERSTANDING AUTOMATIC VARIABLES 110
Overview 111
$Error Variable 111
$Host and $Profile Variables 113
$Host Variable 113
$Profile Variable 113
$Null Variable 114
Clearing Variables 114
Validating Outputs 115
Object Property Checks 115
Array and Collection Operations 116
Filtering Out $Null Values 116
$PSVersionTable Variable 116
Information in $PSVersionTable 117
Conditional Features 117
Debugging and Logging 118
Identifying the Operating Environment 118
$LastExitCode Variable 119
Basic Usage of $LastExitCode 119
Integrating $LastExitCode 120
Using $LastExitCode with Script Blocks 120
Chained Commands 120

    Logging with $LastExitCode 121
    Troubleshooting and Decision-making 121
$MyInvocation Variable 122
    $MyInvocation for Debugging and Logging 122
    Dynamic Script Behavior 123
    Script Reflection 124
$Args for Script Parameters 124
    $Args in Monitoring Scripts 124
    Sample Program: Passing Parameters 124
    Mixing $Args with Regular Parameters 126
Summary 127

CHAPTER 7: DEBUGGING TECHNIQUES **128**

Debugging Overview 129
Write-Host Cmdlets 130
Write-Error Cmdlet 130
Sample Program: Using Write-Host and Write-Error 132
    Utilizing Write-Host for Feedback and Status 132
    Using Write-Error for Disk Space Alerts 132
    Combining Write-Host and Write-Error for CPU Monitoring 133
    Memory Monitoring with Clear Communication 134
    Key Learnings 134
Using Breakpoints for Effective Debugging 135
    Overview 135
    Setting Breakpoints 135
    Working with Breakpoints During Debugging 136
    Managing Breakpoints 136
Debugging in Remote Sessions 137
    Establishing Remote Session 138
    Enter and Exit Remote Session 138
    Enable Remote Debugging 138
    Executing and Debugging Remotely 139

  Closing the Loop 139
Debugging Tools 140
  ISE Debugger..140
  Variables Pane 141
  Sample Program: Using ISE Debugger and Variables Pane................................141
Decoding Stack Traces 142
  Understanding Stack Trace 142
  Sample Program: Analyzing Stack Traces 143
  Decoding the Trace..144
Summary 145

CHAPTER 8: WORKING WITH WHILE LOOPS **146**
Essence of While Loops 147
Syntax and Structure 148
  Basic Syntax...148
  Compound Conditions 149
  Do-While 149
  $? Variable 150
  Nesting 'While' Loops..150
  Infinite Loops and Safe Exits 151
  Sample Program: Using While Loops for System Monitoring.............................152
  Retry Mechanisms 153
  Continue Statement...153
Error Handling in While Loops 154
  Possibility of Errors 154
  Managing Errors..154
  Specific Errors 156
  Controlling Error Output 157
Debugging While Loops 158
  Identifying the Problem...158
  Interactive Debugging with Set-PSBreakpoint 158
  Inspecting Variables...159

Log Verbosely 159
Do-While and Do-Until Loops 160
  Do-While Loop 160
  Do-Until Loop 160
  Using in System Monitoring Script 161
Combine Do-While and Do-Until Together 162
  Foundation of Nested Looping 162
  Sample Program: Exploit Nested Looping 162
Loop Control Commands 165
  Break Command 165
  Continue Command 165
  Sample Program: Working of Loop Control 165
Summary 168

CHAPTER 9: MANAGING WINDOWS SYSTEMS 170

Windows Management Overview 171
  Why PowerShell for Windows Management? 171
  A Unified Ecosystem 171
  Scalability, Flexibility and Extensibility 171
User Account Management in WMI 172
  WMI's Role in User Account Management 172
  Leveraging PowerShell for WMI-based Account Management 173
File and Directory Management in WMI 174
  File and Directory Operations via WMI 174
Registry Operations in WMI 175
  Accessing Registry Data with WMI 175
  Writing and Modifying Registry Data 176
  Deleting Registry Keys and Values 176
  Enumerating Registry Keys and Values 177
  Registry Operations Best Practices 177
Service Management in WMI 178
  Role in Service Management 178

Accessing Service Information 178
Controlling Services: Start, Stop, Pause, and Resume 178
Modifying Service Configuration 179
Monitoring Services 179
Service Management Best Practices 180
Event Logs and Diagnostics in WMI 180
Tapping into Event Logs 180
Retrieving Event Log Metadata 181
Reacting to Events with WMI Eventing 181
Clearing Event Logs 182
Centralized Event Log Management 182
Custom Event Triggers 183
Performance Implications and Optimization 183
System Updates and Patches in WMI 184
Win32_QuickFixEngineering Class 184
Sorting and Filtering Updates 185
Remote Patch Management 185
Windows Firewall Management 186
Navigating NetFirewall Namespace 186
Group Policy Management in WMI 188
Accessing RSOP Data 188
Filtering GPOs for Specific Settings 188
Retrieving GPO Details 188
Modifying Group Policy Settings 189
Backup, Import, and Restore Operations 189
Security Filtering and Delegation 190
Summary 190
CHAPTER 10: REMOTE SYSTEMS MANAGEMENT **192**
Remote Management with PowerShell 193
Enabling Remote Management 194
Pre-requisites 194

Setting up Environment 194
Enabling Remoting 195
Adjusting Firewall 195
Verifying Configuration 195
Configuring Remoting and SSL 196
Configuring Trusted Hosts 196
Secure Communication Channels 196
Need for Secure Communication Channels 196
Setting up Secure Communications 197
Managing Sessions in PowerShell 199
What is a PSSession? 199
Creating a New Session 199
Using an Established Session 199
Managing Multiple Sessions 200
Reusing Sessions 200
Disconnecting and Reconnecting Sessions 200
Removing Sessions 201
Setting Session Configuration 201
File Transfer to Remote Systems 201
Why Transfer Files? 201
Cmdlets and Techniques for File Transfer 202
PowerShell and SMB 202
Using BITS (Background Intelligent Transfer Service) 203
PowerShell Remoting Best Practices 203
Use Encrypted Channels 203
Employ JEA 204
Regularly Update and Patch 204
Avoid Hardcoding Credentials 204
Limit Scope of Remoting 204
Validate Inputs and Outputs 205
Keep Audit Logs 205

    Test in Controlled Environment 205
    Avoid Overloading Remote Machines 206
Summary 206
Index 209
Epilogue 210

Preface

A practical handbook, "PowerShell Troubleshooting Guide" is designed to help PowerShell enthusiasts improve their skills and make them more effective in real-world applications. Starting with basic scripting and progressing to comprehensive system expertise, the book explores the immense possibilities of PowerShell.

Beginning with fundamental ideas, readers are exposed to the heart of PowerShell, including its architecture, command structures, and scripting intricacies. Each chapter delves into a specific theme, such as troubleshooting approaches, advanced debugging, loop controls, and robust error-handling systems, ensuring that the reader is well-prepared to face any obstacles that may arise.

One of the book's strongest points is its emphasis on hands-on learning. It gives you hands-on experience automating complex system and Windows administrative operations while demystifying the processes involved. Readers will learn how to establish secure communication channels, manage remote sessions, and transfer files to faraway systems with the help of realistic examples and clear explanations. Combining this remote knowledge with an in-depth examination of debugging, experts will be able to fix any problems with their automation solutions quickly and easily.

Most importantly, this book takes readers on a trip that will elevate them from PowerShell user to PowerShell maestro, allowing them to solve all of their administrative problems in a way that is streamlined, efficient, and imaginative.

In this book you will learn how to:

- Grasp core PowerShell concepts, ensuring a robust base for advanced operations.
- Learn to craft effective scripts, optimizing automation tasks.
- Dive into managing networks remotely, ensuring seamless operations.
- Acquire skills to troubleshoot scripts, ensuring error-free automation.
- Understand Windows Management Instrumentation, linking it with PowerShell.
- Prioritize secure scripting and master remote sessions, ensuring system integrity, connectivity and control.
- Adopt industry-standard best practices for PowerShell.

GitforGits

Prerequisites

This book is intended for the whole PowerShell community and everyone who is required to work with PowerShell in any capacity. This book assumes no prior knowledge and will quickly transform you into a competent, talented, solution-focused, and smart powershell practitioner. Following along with the book only requires a basic understanding of scripting.

Codes Usage

Are you in need of some helpful code examples to assist you in your programming and documentation? Look no further! Our book offers a wealth of supplemental material, including code examples and exercises.

Not only is this book here to aid you in getting your job done, but you have our permission to use the example code in your programs and documentation. However, please note that if you are reproducing a significant portion of the code, we do require you to contact us for permission.

But don't worry, using several chunks of code from this book in your program or answering a question by citing our book and quoting example code does not require permission. But if you do choose to give credit, an attribution typically includes the title, author, publisher, and ISBN. For example, "PowerShell Troubleshooting Guide by Steeve Lee".

If you are unsure whether your intended use of the code examples falls under fair use or the permissions outlined above, please do not hesitate to reach out to us at: support@gitforgits.com.

We are happy to assist and clarify any concerns.

Acknowledgement

I owe GitforGits a significant debt of appreciation for their unwavering excitement and excellent advice during the entire process of writing this book. Their expertise and meticulous editing ensured that the text was accessible to readers of all reading levels and comprehension abilities. Furthermore, I'd want to thank everyone engaged in the publication process for their contributions to making this book a reality. Their efforts, from copyediting to promotion, have helped to shape the initiative into what it is today.

Finally, I want to thank everyone who has showed me unconditional love and encouragement throughout my life. Their assistance was critical in completing this work. I appreciate your assistance with this endeavor as well as your continuous interest in my career.

Chapter 1: Introduction to PowerShell Troubleshooting

Introduction

Current State of PowerShell

PowerShell has come a long way since its inception in 2006. It was originally intended as a task automation and configuration management framework for Windows, but it has since expanded far beyond those confines. The transition from PowerShell v1's monolithic architecture to PowerShell Core's open-source, cross-platform capabilities has been monumental, mirroring the changes in today's IT landscape. With cloud computing becoming more common, PowerShell's versatility is more important than ever.

Administrators had a limited set of tools to manage Windows servers and desktops in the early days of IT infrastructure. They received a powerful, extensible scripting language built on top of the .NET framework with the introduction of PowerShell. PowerShell introduced a plethora of cmdlets—single-function commands built into the shell that can manage everything from file operations to system diagnostics. As a result, IT professionals no longer needed to switch between tools and were able to manage tasks more efficiently directly from the PowerShell environment.

This unified approach has boosted PowerShell's influence in DevOps culture. Continuous integration, continuous delivery (CI/CD), and system monitoring necessitate a plethora of tools and practices for DevOps professionals. PowerShell is an all-in-one solution for these requirements. Its powerful scripting capabilities enable IT professionals to automate repetitive tasks, increasing productivity while decreasing the possibility of human error. For example, a simple PowerShell script can automate virtual machine deployment, storage provisioning, and network configuration management. The use of Desired State Configuration (DSC) allows administrators to define and enforce configurations across multiple platforms, including Linux and macOS, thereby broadening its applicability.

PowerShell's extensibility is another key feature that contributes to its popularity. For enterprise-level applications, the ability to create custom modules and share them across multiple projects is invaluable. Such modularity and reusability offer significant time and cost savings in an era where microservices architecture is becoming the norm. Furthermore, a thriving ecosystem of third-party modules and libraries, available via the PowerShell Gallery, has sprung up to support a wide range of functionalities that go beyond native capabilities.

Integration with cloud computing services, particularly Azure, is one of the key trends indicating PowerShell's influence. Cloud providers, such as Microsoft, are increasingly providing PowerShell cmdlets for managing cloud-based resources. Because of this seamless integration, it is an excellent tool for hybrid cloud environments where resources are shared between on-premise servers and the cloud. For example, the Azure PowerShell module makes it incredibly simple to create and manage Azure Resource Groups, Virtual Networks, and even Kubernetes clusters. This allows IT professionals to manage complex cloud architectures using the same language and syntax that they have become accustomed to.

PowerShell Influence

PowerShell Core, the open-source version of PowerShell, has expanded its capabilities by adding cross-platform support. Its influence extends beyond Azure. With this advancement, IT professionals can now use PowerShell scripts to manage Linux and macOS systems, making it an even more powerful tool in multi-platform environments. This is an important change as businesses shift to a more platform-agnostic approach, allowing them to choose the best tools for specific tasks rather than being limited by operating systems.

Another noteworthy trend is the move toward "infrastructure as code," in which PowerShell plays an important role. Treating infrastructure setup and configurations as code enables IT professionals to version control their configurations, roll back to previous configurations, and automate resource provisioning and de-provisioning. As a result, the entire IT infrastructure becomes more agile, robust, and less prone to manual configuration errors.

As PowerShell becomes more widely used, it is increasingly being used for cybersecurity attacks such as data breaches and ransomware attacks. As a result, today's IT professionals must have a solid understanding of its capabilities, as well as secure practices. PowerShell's integration into the Microsoft ecosystem, such as its inclusion in Windows Terminal, membership in the Sysinternals Suite, and integration with Visual Studio Code, adds another layer to its ubiquity and fosters a collaborative environment in which developers and IT professionals can collaborate, resulting in faster development cycles and streamlined management processes.

Challenges and Issues

While PowerShell has undeniably established itself as a cornerstone in the world of IT and DevOps, it is not without its challenges and limitations.

Script Complexity and Scalability

As your PowerShell scripts grow in size and complexity, maintaining and managing them becomes increasingly challenging. Large scripts often mean that more variables, loops, and conditions are in play, making it difficult to identify the root cause when something goes wrong. You might use Write-Debug, Write-Verbose, or even create custom logging to troubleshoot issues, but when a script spans hundreds or thousands of lines of code, tracing a problem back to its source is no small feat. This book will dive deep into effective debugging strategies to tackle such issues, including using PowerShell's built-in debugging features and leveraging specialized debugging tools in the PowerShell ISE.

Security Concerns

PowerShell's versatility and capabilities also make it a tool for exploitation if not adequately secured. Cybercriminals use PowerShell to execute malicious code as it provides them the ability to interact directly with the operating system and its core functionalities. Security modules and logging features can help identify and prevent these security threats. A critical understanding of execution policies, the use of signed scripts, and other best practices can go a long way in securing your PowerShell environment. This book provides a detailed look at PowerShell's security model and offers guidelines for securing your scripts and environment.

Cross-Platform Challenges
With the advent of PowerShell Core, cross-platform scripting is now a reality. However, transitioning from Windows PowerShell to PowerShell Core brings its own set of challenges, such as compatibility issues. While PowerShell Core aims to be a drop-in replacement for Windows PowerShell, not all modules and cmdlets are compatible. You might find yourself re-writing or adapting existing Windows-only scripts to ensure they work in a Linux or macOS environment. This book will help you navigate these transitions by providing comprehensive guides on the cmdlets and modules that work cross-platform, along with alternatives for those that don't.

Managing Remote Sessions
PowerShell remoting is undeniably powerful but is fraught with complexities, especially when dealing with multiple remote sessions concurrently. Handling credentials securely, managing session states, and transmitting data in a serialized format are some of the hurdles that developers often encounter. In a network where firewalls, different operating systems, and varying permissions levels coexist, remoting can become a complex beast to master. This book will explore methods for secure, effective, and efficient remoting.

Automation Pitfalls
Automating tasks with PowerShell can sometimes lead to over-automation, where human intervention could be more effective. It might be tempting to script out every aspect of your daily tasks, but automation should be employed thoughtfully. Too much automation can lead to scripts that are challenging to debug and manage. Furthermore, automation scripts can sometimes execute unwanted actions too quickly for anyone to intervene, leading to unintended consequences. Therefore, there is a need to strike a balance, a topic this book will cover exhaustively.

Versioning and Updates
Keeping up with new versions and updates is crucial in any software development cycle, more so in PowerShell, which has moved from a Windows-only environment to a cross-platform tool. This results in versioning issues, where a script that works perfectly in one environment may fail in another due to cmdlet changes or deprecated features. This book will provide you with the knowledge to manage different PowerShell versions effectively and ensure your scripts are compatible across various platforms.

Workflow Orchestration

DevOps professionals often find themselves orchestrating complex workflows that involve various tools and platforms. PowerShell is commonly used for such orchestration but can become unwieldy when the workflows are exceptionally complex or require integration with non-Windows or cloud-native tools. Learning how to use PowerShell in conjunction with tools like Jenkins, Kubernetes, or Terraform for orchestrated, multi-step workflows is a topic that this book will cover, offering solutions for more complex IT operations tasks.

Troubleshooting in the Cloud

PowerShell's capabilities extend into cloud management, mainly through services like Azure. However, managing resources in the cloud presents a different set of challenges, like network latency, API rate limits, and managing state in a stateless environment. Given that PowerShell can manipulate cloud resources directly, improper usage or errors can lead to unintended costs or expose security vulnerabilities. The chapters in this book related to cloud management will cover these issues in depth, providing strategies for effective and safe cloud resource management using PowerShell.

Real-World Adaptability

Learning PowerShell in a controlled environment is one thing; applying it in the real world is another. DevOps professionals and PowerShell developers often find that tutorials and guides do not always translate directly into practical application. Scenarios in the real world often involve nuances and exceptions that standard guides and documentation may not cover. This book will focus on real-world examples and case studies, thereby preparing you for the challenges you might face in an actual work environment.

This book aims to be a comprehensive resource for PowerShell developers and DevOps professionals by not just understanding the how-to but also the why and what-if, which are crucial for troubleshooting and mastering PowerShell in complex IT ecosystems.

Setting up PowerShell on Windows

Installing PowerShell on a Windows system can be approached in multiple ways, each with its own set of steps, advantages, and considerations. For the purpose of this book, the focus will be on installing PowerShell Core, which is the open-source, cross-platform edition. PowerShell Core allows you to manage a variety of systems including Windows, Linux, and macOS, thus offering greater flexibility than Windows PowerShell.

Before you begin the installation process, ensure that your system meets the following requirements:

- Operating System: Windows 8.1 or Windows 10; Windows Server 2012 R2, 2016, or 2019.

- .NET Core 2.x SDK or later.

Option #1: Direct Download from GitHub

For those seeking the most recent features and updates, directly downloading PowerShell from GitHub is an excellent choice. Following steps will direct you to install it directly from github:

- Go to the GitHub releases page for PowerShell, found at: https://github.com/PowerShell/PowerShell/releases

  - This page is your portal to all the latest versions, each bundled with unique enhancements and bug fixes.

  - On the releases page, you'll find a range of files. Identify the MSI (Microsoft Installer) package that matches your computer's architecture: look for either x64 (for 64-bit systems) or x86 (for 32-bit systems). These MSI packages are tailored for seamless integration with Windows environments.

  - After downloading the MSI file, locate it in your downloads folder or wherever it is saved.

  - Double-click this file to initiate the installation wizard, a straightforward interface guiding you through the setup. The installer will prompt you with several options. Each screen allows you to customize aspects of the installation. You can choose the installation directory, decide whether to add PowerShell to the system path (which allows you to run it from any directory in the Command Prompt), and configure other settings.

  - A critical step involves options like adding PowerShell to your environment path, which enhances accessibility, and enabling PowerShell remoting for advanced management tasks. For instance, enabling PowerShell remoting is beneficial for remote system management and automation tasks.

  - Once you've set your preferences, click "Install" to begin the installation process. The installer will proceed to install PowerShell on your system, which might take a few moments.

  - To confirm a successful installation, open a new command prompt or terminal. Type pwsh and press Enter. This command launches PowerShell. If installed correctly, the prompt changes, indicating you're now in a PowerShell environment, ready to execute PowerShell commands.

Option #2: Using Package Manager

If you prefer using package managers for software installations, both Windows Package Manager (Winget) and Chocolatey offer straightforward ways to install PowerShell Core.

Using Windows Package Manager
- Open Command Prompt as Administrator: Right-click the Start menu and select "Command Prompt (Admin)" to open a command prompt with administrative privileges.

- Run the Command: Type winget install --name PowerShell --exact and press Enter. The package manager will take care of the download and installation.

Using Chocolatey
- Install Chocolatey: If you don't have Chocolatey installed, you'll need to install it first. Open an administrative Command Prompt and run:

Set-ExecutionPolicy Bypass -Scope Process -Force; iex ((New-Object System.Net.WebClient).DownloadString('https://chocolatey.org/install.ps1'))

- Install PowerShell Core: Type choco install powershell-core and press Enter.

Option #3: Using PowerShell Deployment Toolkit

PowerShell Deployment Toolkit (PSDT) is a set of PowerShell scripts for installing software silently. For large-scale deployments or installations on multiple machines, this is the preferred method and can be undertaken as below:

- Go to the GitHub repository for PowerShell Deployment Toolkit and download the source code.

- Customize the XML Configuration: The toolkit uses an XML file to understand what software to install. Update this file to include PowerShell Core.

- Run Installer Script: Execute the installation script from an elevated PowerShell prompt. This will install PowerShell Core on the system according to the specifications in the XML configuration.

- Regardless of the installation method used, you'll want to update the PowerShell Core help system. Open PowerShell Core and run the following command:

Update-Help

- This will download and install the latest help files, ensuring that you have the most up-to-date documentation available within the PowerShell environment.

You may follow any of the above 3 options to install powershell but keep in mind that different installation methods offer flexibility and allows you to choose the most convenient or suitable approach to reach your desired milestones.

Update PowerShell Core

PowerShell Core must be updated on a regular basis to maintain its effectiveness and security. Regular updates are an important practice in effective system management, providing not only security benefits but also access to the most recent technological advancements in PowerShell Core. This procedure ensures that you are taking advantage of the most recent advancements in features, enjoying improved performance, and receiving critical security updates.

Option #1: Via GitHub

Before updating, it's good to know which version you're currently running. Open PowerShell Core and run:

$PSVersionTable.PSVersion

This command will display the current version.

Navigate to the GitHub releases page for PowerShell at:
https://github.com/PowerShell/PowerShell/releases

Download the MSI package for the new version that suits your system architecture (x64 or x86).

Go to Control Panel, then Programs, then Programs and Features, find PowerShell Core in the list, and uninstall it. And this won't affect your scripts, modules, or configurations.

Double-click on the downloaded MSI package and follow the installation prompts as outlined in the installation section. Once installed, verify by running $PSVersionTable.PSVersion again to see if it displays the new version.

Option #2: Via Package Manager

If you initially installed PowerShell Core using a package manager like Windows Package Manager (Winget) or Chocolatey, you can also use them to update it.

Using Windows Package Manager
- Open Command Prompt and you can access this by right-clicking the Start menu and selecting "Command Prompt (Admin)".

- Run winget upgrade --name PowerShell --exact. The package manager will find the new version, download it, and replace the old one automatically.

Using Chocolatey
- Open and access the command prompt in the same way as described in the option #1.

- Type choco upgrade powershell-core and press Enter. Chocolatey will handle the update process, including uninstalling the old version and installing the new one.

Option #3: Using MSI

Some newer versions of the MSI installer for PowerShell Core offer in-place upgrades. This means you can install the new version without needing to uninstall the old one.

Just go to the GitHub releases page and download the new MSI.

Double-click the downloaded MSI package. If in-place upgrades are supported, the installer will automatically replace the old version with the new one.

Option #4: Using PowerShell Script

If you frequently update PowerShell Core, you can automate this process using a PowerShell script.

Create or download a PowerShell script designed to automate the upgrade process. This script would typically use web cmdlets like Invoke-WebRequest to download the latest MSI from GitHub and then use Start-Process to run the installer.

Simply execute this script in PowerShell Core when you wish to update. Ensure you are running it with administrative privileges so that it can handle installation tasks.

After updating, it's advisable to refresh the help files to ensure that you have the latest documentation. Open PowerShell Core and execute:

Update-Help

You may also want to check that all your essential modules and custom scripts are working as expected in the new version. Run some tests or execute commonly used commands to ensure compatibility.

PowerShell ISE

The PowerShell Integrated Scripting Environment (ISE) is a graphical user interface (GUI)-based host application that allows for the creation of scripts and modules. It provides a feature-rich environment with syntax highlighting, tab completion, and advanced debugging. It is important to note, however, that PowerShell ISE is not available for PowerShell Core; it is only compatible with Windows PowerShell. So, for those who prefer Windows PowerShell, simply follow the steps outlined below to install ISE.

But before you attempt to install ISE, it's a good idea to check if it's already installed on your system.

- Open Windows PowerShell (not PowerShell Core) by searching for it in the Start Menu.
- Type Get-Command ISE and press Enter.
- If you see output, ISE is already installed. If you see no output, you need to install it.

Installing ISE via Windows Features

To install ISE using Windows Features:

- Open Control Panel, then go to "Programs and Features".
- Click "Turn Windows features on or off" on the left.
- Find "Windows PowerShell Integrated Scripting Environment" in the list and check its box.
- Click "OK" to install ISE. Windows will add the needed files.

Launching ISE

- After installation, search for "PowerShell ISE" in the Start menu and click on it to launch.

- Alternatively, you can also launch ISE from the command line by typing powershell_ise.exe and pressing Enter.

Understanding ISE Interface

ISE is divided into three primary panes:

Script Pane

This is where you'll write and edit your scripts. It's a full-featured text editor made specifically for scripting. Syntax highlighting is a key feature of the Script Pane, which makes your code more readable by coloring different elements (such as commands, parameters, and strings) in different colors. This not only makes it easier to write code more efficiently, but it also makes troubleshooting easier by making it easier to spot errors or anomalies in your script.

Console Pane

The Console Pane works similarly to a traditional PowerShell console. This is the part of ISE where you can run individual PowerShell commands. Consider it a proving ground for commands before incorporating them into your scripts in the Script Pane. The Console Pane is especially useful for quick command execution and checking command outputs on the fly.

Output Pane

The Output Pane displays the results of any scripts or individual commands that you run. This pane is essential for inspecting the results of your code and commands. It displays what your script is doing or the results of your commands. If there are any errors or warnings, they will also be shown here. The Output Pane is extremely useful for debugging because it allows you to see the immediate impact of your code and make necessary changes.

Basic Customizations

Customization of Fonts and Colors

To personalize your scripting environment, you can change the fonts and colors. To do so, go to the menu bar and select "Tools," then "Options" from the dropdown menu. This will bring up the Options dialog box. This window contains settings for the appearance of the text and background in the various panes. The font style, size, and color, as well as the background color, are all editable. These tweaks can help make the scripting environment more eye-friendly, especially if you spend a lot of time scripting.

Scripting Pane Layout Configuration

You can change the layout of the Script Pane to suit your needs. The Script Pane is by default positioned above the Console Pane, but this can be changed. You can change the order of the Script Pane and the Console Pane in the View menu. Select "Show Script Pane Right" from the

"View" menu. The Script Pane will be moved to the right side of the Console Pane, providing a side-by-side view. This layout is especially useful if you want to see more of your script at once or prefer a larger view for your Console Pane.

Debugging Features

Setting Breakpoints

Breakpoints are an essential part of debugging in any programming environment, including PowerShell ISE. Simply right-click on the line of code where you want to pause execution to set a breakpoint in your script. Then, from the context menu, choose "Toggle Breakpoint". A breakpoint will be placed on that line, which will be visually denoted by a red dot or a highlighted line. When you run the script, the execution will pause at this breakpoint, allowing you to inspect variable states, script flow, and identify any issues or bugs at that specific point in the code.

Step-through Debugging

Another useful debugging feature in ISE is step-through debugging. This allows you to run your script one line at a time, which can be extremely useful in determining where things are going wrong. Step-by-step debugging can be accessed via the debugging toolbar or the Debug menu. Stepping into functions or scripts (executing one line and then pausing), stepping over (executing the next line of code but not stepping into any function calls on that line), and stepping out (continuing execution until the current function returns) are all buttons on the toolbar. You can use these tools to closely monitor how each component of your script behaves and how data is manipulated during the execution process.

Modules and Add-ons

Importing Modules

You can improve your scripting capabilities in PowerShell ISE by importing various modules. PowerShell modules are collections of commands, such as cmdlets, functions, variables, and others, that you can use in your scripts. To import a module, run the Import-Module cmdlet followed by the module's name. If you need to work with Active Directory, for example, you can load the ActiveDirectory module by running Import-Module ActiveDirectory in the Console Pane. This cmdlet makes all ActiveDirectory module commands available in your ISE session, allowing you to perform a wide range of Active Directory management tasks.

ISE Add-ons

PowerShell ISE supports add-ons or extensions that can greatly expand its functionality. These add-ons may include new features, improved user interfaces, new cmdlets, or improved integration with other software and services. To install an add-on, use the Install-Module cmdlet, which can be found in the ISE's Console Pane. This cmdlet retrieves and installs the module from the PowerShell Gallery, an online repository of PowerShell content. For example, if you discover an add-on that enhances script editing features or adds extra debugging tools, you can easily add it to your ISE environment to improve your scripting workflow.

ISE Profiles

PowerShell ISE has its own profile script, separate from the PowerShell console. This allows you to run specific startup scripts when ISE launches.

- Locate Profile: Use $profile to find the location of your ISE profile script.

- Create/Edit Profile: If the profile script doesn't exist, you can create one. Edit this script to include any startup operations you'd like ISE to perform.

Working with Remote Sessions

You can use ISE to connect to remote PowerShell sessions using the New-PSSession cmdlet and then importing it with Import-PSSession. This allows you to execute commands on remote systems directly from ISE.

ISE offers an incredibly robust and feature-rich environment for script development and debugging in Windows PowerShell. Although it doesn't support PowerShell Core, its advanced capabilities make it a go-to choice for many Windows-based PowerShell developers.

Navigate PowerShell ISE

Navigating through PowerShell ISE can feel like piloting a spaceship with a multitude of controls, especially if you're not familiar with IDEs (Integrated Development Environments). Understanding how to effectively navigate and utilize the various features in ISE can dramatically improve your productivity and script development experience.

Menu Bar and Toolbar

The Menu Bar and Toolbar at the top provide quick access to many commands and settings. You can save scripts, open files, debug, and perform various other tasks from here. If you hover your mouse over each icon, you'll see tooltips that describe what each button does.

Keyboard Shortcuts

Mastering keyboard shortcuts can save you a lot of time. Following are some critical ones:

- F5: Run the entire script.

- F8: Run only the selected lines.
- Ctrl+J: Brings up a snippet menu, allowing you to insert common code blocks.
- Ctrl+Space: Autocomplete suggestions for cmdlets or variables.

Tab Expansion

In the Script and Console Panes, you can use tab completion to speed up the typing of cmdlet names, paths, and variable names. For example, typing Get-Pr and pressing the Tab key will cycle through all cmdlets starting with Get-Pr.

Snippets

Snippets are small blocks of reusable code. Access them by hitting Ctrl+J or right-clicking and choosing "Start Snippets." These can be everything from a simple ForEach loop to more complex structures like a Switch statement. You can even create your own custom snippets.

Context Menu

Right-clicking inside the Script Pane will reveal a context menu, offering you the ability to insert snippets, run selection, or even set breakpoints for debugging.

Variable Explorer

If you navigate to View > Show Command Add-on, you will notice a sidebar appear that contains a 'Variables' tab. This is a fantastic way to keep track of the variables currently in the session scope. Double-clicking a variable will let you edit its value on the fly.

Command Add-on

The Command Add-on pane shows a list of cmdlets, functions, workflows, and even your own custom functions. You can browse through this list, double-click any command to insert it into your script, and fill out parameter values in a form-like interface below the list.

Output Pane Customizations

You can customize the Output Pane by right-clicking inside it. Options include the ability to clear the display, select all text, and even save the current output to a txt or xml file.

Error List and Output List

Below the Output Pane, you will find tabs for 'Errors' and 'Output List'. Errors list will show all errors in your script, making it easier to debug. The Output List displays details about your script runs.

Script Tabs

If you are working on multiple scripts simultaneously, each script opens in a new tab within the Script Pane. You can switch between them effortlessly, which is especially useful for comparing scripts or copying elements from one to another.

Context Highlighting

When you select a bracket, its corresponding pair gets highlighted, helping you ensure that each opening bracket has a matching closing one. This feature is particularly useful for nested loops and conditional statements.

Find and Replace

The Ctrl+F shortcut opens the 'Find' dialogue, and Ctrl+H opens the 'Replace' dialogue. These features are incredibly useful for locating specific strings or variables and replacing them en masse, saving you the effort of manual searching and editing.

Debugging Pane

If you activate debugging mode, a new pane opens at the bottom, which allows you to monitor variables closely, step into functions, and even change variable values in real-time.

Remote Tab

In the toolbar, you will see an icon for opening a new remote PowerShell tab. This is a convenient way to establish and manage remote sessions directly within ISE, without having to manually enter session-related cmdlets in the console pane.

Knowing your way around PowerShell ISE will make you more proficient in scripting, debugging, and executing PowerShell commands, all of which make good use of the extensive feature set of PowerShell. The environment may appear intimidating at first, but with a little practice, you'll find it incredibly supportive for all of your scripting needs.

Essential PowerShell Commands

Learning the key PowerShell commands is like acquiring the fundamental building blocks for a versatile toolkit. Knowing how to utilize these commands can not only speed up routine tasks but also unlock powerful functionalities.

Get-Command

The basic syntax for the Get-Command cmdlet is Get-Command [-Name] <String[]>. This cmdlet is used to retrieve information about the commands available in your PowerShell session. The -Name parameter is optional and it specifies the name of the commands you want to retrieve. You can use wildcards to specify multiple commands.

For example, if you run Get-Command Get-* in PowerShell ISE or in a PowerShell console, the command will list all cmdlets, functions, workflows, and aliases available on your system that start with the prefix "Get-". This is incredibly useful for discovering commands or for finding a specific command when you only remember part of its name.

By default, Get-Command retrieves all types of commands, including cmdlets, functions, workflows, and aliases. However, you can refine your search. For instance, if you only want to list cmdlets, you can use the -CommandType parameter like Get-Command -CommandType Cmdlet Get-*. Another powerful feature of Get-Command is its ability to list commands from a specific module. By using the -Module parameter, you can view all the commands that are part of a particular module. For example, Get-Command -Module ActiveDirectory would list all commands in the ActiveDirectory module. Get-Command not only lists commands but also provides key information about them, such as their type, module name, and definition. This can be extremely helpful for understanding what a command does and how it can be used in your scripts.

Get-Help

The Get-Help cmdlet is a fundamental tool in PowerShell that provides detailed information about PowerShell commands, including cmdlets, functions, scripts, and workflows. The basic syntax for using Get-Help is Get-Help <Command-Name>. You simply replace <Command-Name> with the name of the command you want information about. For example, Get-Help Get-Service will provide detailed information about the Get-Service cmdlet.

Just like with Get-Command, you can use wildcards with Get-Help to get information about multiple commands that match a pattern. For instance, Get-Help Get-* will provide help topics for all commands that start with "Get-". When you run Get-Help for a specific command, it typically returns a detailed overview, including a description of what the command does, its syntax, a list of parameters with descriptions, and often some examples of how to use the command. If you're looking for practical examples of how to use a command, you can use the -Examples parameter. For instance, Get-Help Get-Service -Examples will show examples of how to use the Get-Service cmdlet.

Sometimes the help files on your system might not be up-to-date. You can use the -Online parameter to open the latest version of the help file in your default web browser. For example, Get-Help Get-Service -Online will take you to the online documentation for Get-Service.

Get-Process

The Get-Process cmdlet in PowerShell is used to retrieve information about the processes running on a computer. It is a versatile tool for monitoring and managing system processes. The simplest way to use Get-Process is by typing Get-Process without any parameters. This command lists all the currently running processes on your computer, along with basic information such as their process ID, CPU usage, memory usage, and process name.

You can specify one or more process names to Get-Process to retrieve information about only those processes. For example, Get-Process explorer will provide details about the process named 'explorer'. Get-Process also supports wildcards. For instance, Get-Process svchost* will list all processes that start with 'svchost'. To view more detailed information about a process, you can pipe the output of Get-Process to the Format-List cmdlet. For example, Get-Process explorer | Format-List * displays all available details about the 'explorer' process.

Get-Service

The Get-Service cmdlet is used to retrieve information about the services on a local or remote machine. It provides details about the status, display name, and service name of system services. When you run Get-Service without any parameters, it lists all the services installed on your computer, showing their status (Running, Stopped, etc.), display name, and service name.

You can specify the name of a service to get information about that particular service. For example, Get-Service -Name wuauserv provides details about the Windows Update service. Similar to other PowerShell cmdlets, Get-Service supports the use of wildcards. For instance, Get-Service -Name 'w*' will list all services whose names start with the letter 'w'. You can filter services based on their status. For example, Get-Service | Where-Object {$_.Status -eq 'Running'} lists all services that are currently running. To see more detailed information about a service, you can use the Format-List cmdlet. For example, Get-Service wuauserv | Format-List * will show all the properties of the Windows Update service.

Set-ExecutionPolicy

The Set-ExecutionPolicy cmdlet is used to determine the execution policy for PowerShell scripts on your system. This policy helps control the level of security surrounding script execution, restricting or allowing the running of PowerShell scripts based on where they come from and whether they are signed by a trusted publisher. The basic command syntax is Set-ExecutionPolicy <PolicyName>, where <PolicyName> is the desired execution policy level as below:

- Restricted: This is the default policy. It does not allow any scripts to run.

- AllSigned: Scripts can run only if they are signed by a trusted publisher

- RemoteSigned: Scripts downloaded from the internet must be signed by a trusted publisher; locally created scripts can run without being signed.

- Unrestricted: Runs scripts regardless of their origin and whether they are signed. However, it warns the user before running scripts from untrusted sources.

- Bypass: Nothing is blocked and no warnings are displayed.

- Default: Sets the default execution policy defined by Windows.

To set an execution policy, you would use a command like Set-ExecutionPolicy RemoteSigned. This command sets the policy to allow locally created scripts to run while ensuring scripts from the internet are signed by a trusted publisher.

Import-Module

The Import-Module cmdlet is used to add PowerShell modules into your current session. A module is a package that contains PowerShell cmdlets, providers, functions, workflows, variables, and aliases. By importing a module, you gain access to these additional commands and functionalities. The basic syntax is Import-Module <ModuleName>, where <ModuleName> is the name of the module you want to import. For example, Import-Module ActiveDirectory would load the ActiveDirectory module, making its cmdlets and functions available in your session. If the module is not in a default path where PowerShell looks for modules, you can specify the full path to the module file. For example, Import-Module C:\Path\To\Your\Module.psm1.

Some modules may have aliases that you can use instead of the full module name, making it quicker and easier to import them. Also, you can import only specific commands from a module using the -Cmdlet or -Function parameters. For example, Import-Module ActiveDirectory -Cmdlet Get-ADUser will import only the Get-ADUser cmdlet from the ActiveDirectory module.

New-Item

The New-Item cmdlet is used for creating new items, such as files, directories, registry keys, or even variables in PowerShell. It's a versatile command that helps in various scripting and system management tasks. The basic syntax for creating a new item is New-Item -Path <Path> -ItemType <Type> -Name <Name>, where <Path> is the location where you want to create the item, <Type> is the type of the item (e.g., file, directory), and <Name> is the name of the new item.

For example, to create a new directory, you would use New-Item -Path "C:\ExamplePath" -ItemType Directory -Name "NewFolder". Similarly, to create a new file, you would use New-Item -Path "C:\ExamplePath\NewFolder" -ItemType File -Name "NewFile.txt". New-Item also allows you to specify additional properties like content for files. For example, New-Item -Path "C:\ExamplePath\NewFile.txt" -ItemType File -Value "This is some text" creates a text file with the specified content.

Remove-Item

The Remove-Item cmdlet is used to delete items, such as files, directories, registry keys, or variables in PowerShell. It's an essential command for managing and cleaning up files and directories. The basic syntax for deleting an item is Remove-Item -Path <Path>, where <Path> is the location of the item you want to delete.

For example, to delete a file, you would use Remove-Item -Path "C:\ExamplePath\NewFolder\NewFile.txt". To delete a directory and all its contents, you would use Remove-Item -Path "C:\ExamplePath\NewFolder" -Recurse, where -Recurse is used to indicate that all contents inside the folder should also be removed. Remove-Item includes safety features like -WhatIf and -Confirm. The -WhatIf parameter simulates the deletion so you can see what would happen without actually performing the deletion. The -Confirm parameter prompts you for confirmation before deleting each item.

Test-Connection

The Test-Connection cmdlet in PowerShell is similar to the traditional ping command. It's used to send Internet Control Message Protocol (ICMP) echo request packets to a target host and receive echo replies to test the connection, latency, and packet loss to that host. The basic syntax is Test-Connection -TargetName <HostName/IP>, where <HostName/IP> is the name or IP address of the target host. For example, Test-Connection -TargetName www.google.com sends echo requests to Google's server. You can specify parameters such as -Count to define the number of echo requests to send, or -BufferSize to set the size of the request packet.

Test-Connection returns information such as the target's IP address, response time for each echo request, and packet loss if any. This cmdlet is commonly used for network troubleshooting, verifying connectivity to remote systems, and measuring network performance.

ConvertTo-Json

The ConvertTo-Json cmdlet converts .NET objects into their JSON (JavaScript Object Notation) representation. This cmdlet is particularly useful for preparing data for web services or for readability. The syntax is ConvertTo-Json -InputObject <Object>, where <Object> is the object you want to convert to JSON format. For example, Get-Process | ConvertTo-Json would take the output of the Get-Process cmdlet and convert it into a JSON format.

You can use the -Depth parameter to specify how many levels of contained objects should be converted. This is important for handling complex objects with nested properties. The cmdlet also supports formatting the output with indentation for better readability using the -Compress parameter. ConvertTo-Json is commonly used in scenarios where there is a need to serialize PowerShell output for web APIs, save data in a human-readable format, or for configuration files.

Each of these above commands embodies the versatility and power of PowerShell. They have been selected based on their broad applicability and utility across a wide range of tasks—from system administration and file management to network monitoring and data manipulation.

PowerShell in Cloud

PowerShell has not been left behind in the paradigm shift from on-premises to cloud computing. PowerShell's capabilities go far beyond local and remote Windows management and into the realm of cloud services. Because of its integration with cloud platforms such as Microsoft Azure, AWS, and Google Cloud, administrators can manage cloud resources just as efficiently as they do local resources.

PowerShell and Microsoft Azure

Azure and PowerShell are like a match made in heaven. Azure provides Azure PowerShell, a module offering cmdlets to manage Azure directly from the PowerShell command line. Azure PowerShell is designed to be a first-class citizen in the PowerShell ecosystem. With cmdlets like New-AzResourceGroup, Get-AzVM, and Set-AzAppServicePlan, you can perform a myriad of Azure operations. You can create virtual machines, manage networks, databases, and even use AI services. PowerShell is deeply integrated into Azure DevOps as well, offering cmdlets for CI/CD pipeline management.

AWS Tools for PowerShell

Amazon Web Services (AWS) also provides robust support for PowerShell through the AWS Tools for PowerShell. This allows users to manage their AWS services directly from the PowerShell console. The module includes a full range of AWS-specific cmdlets to manage all aspects of AWS, including EC2 instances, S3 buckets, and RDS databases. Commands like Get-EC2Instance and New-S3Bucket make these tasks straightforward.

Google Cloud PowerShell

Google Cloud also has a PowerShell SDK, allowing you to manage Google Cloud resources directly from PowerShell. The cmdlets for Google Cloud cover a range of services, including Google Compute Engine, Google Storage, and Google SQL. With the PowerShell SDK for Google Cloud, administrators can automate deployments and manage resources efficiently.

Multi-Cloud Management

For enterprises employing a multi-cloud strategy, PowerShell becomes an even more valuable tool. With modules and cmdlets that can interact with multiple cloud providers, administrators don't have to juggle different toolsets for different platforms. This helps standardize operational procedures across a multi-cloud environment.

Cloud Automation and Scripting

One of the most powerful aspects of using PowerShell in a cloud environment is automation. Cloud services often involve repetitive tasks like provisioning, scaling, and backups. PowerShell scripts can automate these tasks, saving time and minimizing errors. These scripts can be triggered by various events or set to run at specific times, providing highly dynamic, responsive cloud resource management.

Infrastructure as Code (IaC)

With cloud platforms offering Infrastructure as Code services like Azure Resource Manager, AWS CloudFormation, and Google Cloud Deployment Manager, PowerShell fits right in. By utilizing PowerShell scripts, you can version-control your entire infrastructure setup, facilitating collaboration and ensuring reproducibility.

Security and Compliance

PowerShell provides robust options for managing security in the cloud. You can set and manage IAM roles, ensure encryption, and maintain compliance standards. Commands like Get-AzKeyVaultSecret in Azure or Get-IAMUser in AWS provide robust solutions for secure and compliant cloud management.

Monitoring and Logging

Cloud platforms generate vast amounts of data logs and performance metrics. PowerShell can help manage this data. With cmdlets designed to fetch logs, metrics, and even set up alerts, administrators can effectively monitor cloud resources. You can use these cmdlets to integrate with monitoring solutions like Azure Monitor, AWS CloudWatch, or even third-party services.

Cost Management

The elasticity of cloud resources comes with the complexity of cost management. PowerShell can help here, too. You can use it to fetch billing information, set up alerts for cost thresholds, or even automate the de-provisioning of resources when they are not in use to save costs.

Summary

We began this chapter by learning the significance and dominance of PowerShell in today's IT landscape. Recognizing its versatility, we delved into its various challenges, emphasizing that while PowerShell is powerful, it has its own set of issues that professionals face, such as a steep learning curve and security concerns. Practical steps for installing PowerShell Core on Windows were laid out, followed by a practical walkthrough on updating it, to provide users with the foundational knowledge. The chapter then delves into installing and navigating PowerShell ISE, which is essential for effectively writing and debugging scripts.

Following that, the top ten essential commands were examined, each chosen for its broad applicability in both everyday tasks and specialized operations. Get-Command, Get-Help, and Set-ExecutionPolicy are the foundational commands for any PowerShell user, allowing them to interact, manipulate, and retrieve information from their systems with ease. Along with these essential commands, the chapter included practical examples of how to execute each command, which enriched the user's comprehension and provided a quick way to test their understanding.

The final section of the chapter moved from local to cloud environments, emphasizing PowerShell's importance in cloud management. Its integration with Microsoft Azure, AWS, and Google Cloud enables administrators and DevOps professionals to automate tasks, streamline cloud-based operations, and ensure security compliance. PowerShell's multi-cloud management capabilities, Infrastructure as Code, and robust security options demonstrate its adaptability and importance in cloud computing.

This chapter provides you with a thorough understanding of PowerShell's role on local systems as well as in cloud computing, as well as its challenges and essentials. They are better prepared to use PowerShell's capabilities for efficient system management, whether on-premises or in the cloud, armed with this foundational knowledge, practical installation guides, and key commands.

Chapter 2: Understanding PowerShell Command-Line Tools

Command-Line Tools

In this Chapter, the author lays the groundwork for an in-depth exploration of PowerShell's array of command-line tools. These tools cover a wide range of functionalities, including but not limited to: troubleshooting, system monitoring, file operations, text manipulation, and the use of shortcuts and aliases for efficiency. These tools not only extend PowerShell's native capabilities, but also its reach into other operating systems and services.

PowerShell command-line tools are the front-line warriors in troubleshooting. These tools, which are frequently distributed as cmdlets, enable diagnostics, error logging, and event tracking. They enable administrators to pinpoint problems, providing critical information about the system's health. Test-Connection, for example, can be your go-to cmdlet for troubleshooting network latency or connectivity issues.

PowerShell provides a variety of tools for network operations, ranging from basic ping tests to complex network configurations. Get-NetIPAddress and Test-NetConnection commands provide detailed information on network interfaces and connections. These are extremely useful in large-scale network management and in diagnosing network-related issues. Another area where PowerShell excels is system monitoring. Get-Process, Get-Service, and Get-EventLog cmdlets return real-time and historical information about system performance, active services, and system events. This data is necessary for proactive maintenance, system audits, and even reactive troubleshooting.

PowerShell provides a robust set of tools for file operations that go beyond simple file manipulation. You have access to functions for searching, reading, writing, and editing files or folders. Get-Content, Set-Content, Move-Item, and Remove-Item commands form a comprehensive toolset for file management tasks. Text manipulation is frequently overlooked, but it is critical for tasks such as data parsing, log file analysis, and even basic string operations. The Select-String, Replace, and other string manipulation cmdlets in PowerShell are as powerful as any text-processing tool, providing functionality similar to traditional Unix tools like grep, sed, and awk.

Finally, aliases and shortcuts in PowerShell are more than just conveniences; they boost productivity. These features, whether you're creating custom aliases for long commands or using built-in shortcuts like ls for Get-ChildItem, speed up your workflow and make complex operations manageable. As we progress through this chapter, we will go over each of these topics in greater depth, giving you the knowledge and skills you need to fully utilize PowerShell's command-line tools.

File Operations

PowerShell provides a robust toolkit that allows you to do more than just create, delete, and move files. These tools enable complex manipulations ranging from bulk renaming to attribute changes, as well as content editing and complex folder structures. We will investigate each of these cmdlets in depth:

Get-ChildItem

We shall begin with Get-ChildItem, a versatile cmdlet for listing files and directories. It's akin to the ls command in UNIX-based systems. While you can use it simply as Get-ChildItem -Path C:\MyFolder, you can also apply filters.

For example, to list only .txt files, you would run Get-ChildItem -Path C:\MyFolder -Filter *.txt.

New-Item

Creating a new item, be it a directory or a file, can be achieved with New-Item. For instance, New-Item -Path C:\MyFolder -Name NewFile.txt -ItemType File will create a new text file named NewFile.txt inside C:\MyFolder.

Set-Content and Add-Content

Writing to a file involves Set-Content or Add-Content. While Set-Content replaces all the existing data in a file, Add-Content appends data to a file. Given below is how you can append text to an existing file:

Add-Content -Path C:\MyFolder\NewFile.txt -Value 'This is appended text.'

Import-Csv and Export-Csv

When working with CSV files, PowerShell provides specialized cmdlets. You can import a CSV file into a PowerShell object using Import-Csv, manipulate it as you would with any other object, and then write it back using Export-Csv.

For example, importing a CSV file would look something like this:

$data = Import-Csv -Path C:\MyFolder\data.csv

Copy-Item and Move-Item

Copying and moving files are elementary operations but are often involved in complex tasks. For example, you may want to copy all .txt files from one directory to another:

Copy-Item -Path C:\SourceFolder*.txt -Destination C:\DestinationFolder

Rename-Item

Renaming items is as straightforward as invoking Rename-Item. However, in bulk operations, you might use it in a loop. Suppose you have a set of files named File1_old.txt, File2_old.txt, etc., and you want to remove the _old part from all file names:

```
$files = Get-ChildItem -Path C:\MyFolder -Filter *_old.txt
foreach ($file in $files) {
    $newName = $file.Name -replace '_old', ''
    Rename-Item -Path $file.FullName -NewName $newName
}
```

Remove-Item

Deleting files or folders uses Remove-Item. With the -Recurse switch, you can remove a directory and all its subdirectories:

Remove-Item -Path C:\MyFolder\SubFolder -Recurse

Get-FileHash

Another fascinating cmdlet is Get-FileHash, which computes the hash value for a file. This is particularly useful for verifying the integrity of files.

$hash = Get-FileHash -Path C:\MyFolder\MyFile.txt -Algorithm SHA256

Compress-Archive and Expand-Archive

Compressing and decompressing files or folders can be done using Compress-Archive and Expand-Archive. For example, to create a ZIP file:

Compress-Archive -Path C:\MyFolder\MyFile.txt -DestinationPath

C:\MyFolder\MyFile.zip

File Attributes with Get-Item and Set-ItemProperty

File attributes like 'Read-Only' can be read and set using Get-Item and Set-ItemProperty. Following is how you can make a file read-only:

$item = Get-Item -Path C:\MyFolder\MyFile.txt

$item.Attributes = 'ReadOnly'

Network Operations

The above-learned cmdlets cover a wide range of activities, from basic file handling to complex operations like bulk renaming and attribute manipulation. When it comes to network-related tasks, PowerShell also has cmdlets that allow you to manage and troubleshoot network connections, resolve domain names, interact with network protocols, and much more as below:

Test-Connection

Starting off, Test-Connection is the PowerShell equivalent of the classic ping command but with more options. You can specify the count of pings, the buffer size, and more. To ping a server 4 times, you can execute Test-Connection -ComputerName google.com -Count 4.

Test-NetConnection

While Test-Connection checks reachability, Test-NetConnection provides more diagnostic information, including port status, network latency, and routing details. A straightforward check on port 80 for a specific website would look like Test-NetConnection -ComputerName google.com -Port 80.

Get-NetIPAddress

Get-NetIPAddress fetches the IP address configuration of your machine. If you're looking to filter the results to show only IPv4 addresses, you would use Get-NetIPAddress -AddressFamily IPv4.

New-NetIPAddress and Remove-NetIPAddress

If you want to add or remove an IP address, you can use New-NetIPAddress and Remove-NetIPAddress. To assign a new static IP, you might use New-NetIPAddress -IPAddress

192.168.1.2 -PrefixLength 24 -DefaultGateway 192.168.1.1. To remove it, Remove-NetIPAddress -IPAddress 192.168.1.2.

Resolve-DnsName

To resolve a domain name to an IP address or vice versa, you can use Resolve-DnsName. For example, Resolve-DnsName -Name google.com will return the IP addresses associated with that domain.

Get-NetRoute

Examining the routing table can be critical for diagnosing network issues. Get-NetRoute will display the active routes, and you can filter the output to see specific routes based on destination, interface, or other criteria.

Get-NetTCPConnection and Get-NetUDPEndpoint

These cmdlets allow you to see the TCP and UDP connections on your machine. Get-NetTCPConnection gives details like local and remote IP addresses and ports, the connection state, and more.

Similarly, Get-NetUDPEndpoint displays active UDP connections.

Invoke-WebRequest and Invoke-RestMethod

For interacting with HTTP services or APIs, Invoke-WebRequest and Invoke-RestMethod are incredibly useful. The former provides detailed information about the HTTP response, while the latter is more focused on RESTful services and will parse JSON responses automatically.

Get-NetFirewallRule and Set-NetFirewallRule

Managing firewall rules is crucial for network security, and these cmdlets make it easy. With Get-NetFirewallRule, you can list all the rules or filter them based on various criteria. Set-NetFirewallRule allows you to modify existing rules or create new ones.

Armed with the above cmdlets, you can perform a wide range of operations to manage, monitor, and troubleshoot networks. Tasks like pinging a server to check its availability or complex ones like managing firewall rules, PowerShell can do it. This above group of network cmdlets simplifies administrative tasks and bolsters PowerShell's reputation as a comprehensive scripting language.

Advanced Networking Functionalities

PowerShell provides more cmdlets to perform specialized functionalities that can provide granular control and in-depth diagnostics of networks. Following are a couple of cmdlets that you may make use of to perform miscellaneous operations related to the network.

New-NetSwitchTeam

If you want to aggregate multiple network adapters for increased throughput or fault tolerance, New-NetSwitchTeam can come in handy. This cmdlet allows you to create a new NIC team.

For example, New-NetSwitchTeam -Name Team1 -TeamMembers "Ethernet", "Ethernet 2" would create a new NIC team consisting of two adapters named "Ethernet" and "Ethernet 2."

Set-DnsClientServerAddress

This cmdlet allows you to set DNS server addresses for a specific network interface. You can specify both primary and secondary DNS addresses, which is especially useful for complex networking setups. A sample command might be Set-DnsClientServerAddress -InterfaceIndex 12 -ServerAddresses ("10.0.0.1", "10.0.0.2").

Get-NetAdapterBinding

Get-NetAdapterBinding is an advanced cmdlet used for displaying the protocol bindings for network adapters. Each binding allows or disallows certain types of traffic on the network adapter. This command is commonly used in troubleshooting scenarios where you suspect issues with a specific protocol.

Disable-NetAdapterBinding and Enable-NetAdapterBinding

These cmdlets let you disable or enable the protocol bindings for network adapters.

For example, to disable IPv6 on a specific network adapter, you'd use Disable-NetAdapterBinding -Name "Ethernet" -ComponentID ms_tcpip6.

Get-NetNeighbor

This cmdlet provides a way to view the ARP cache, essentially showing you the MAC address to IP address mappings on your local network. This is invaluable for diagnosing duplicate IP issues or for confirming network layer connectivity between hosts.

Get-NetTransportFilter and New-NetTransportFilter

These cmdlets are used for quality of service (QoS) settings on your network. You can view existing transport filters with Get-NetTransportFilter and create new ones using New-NetTransportFilter.

For example, you could create a filter to prioritize SSH traffic with New-NetTransportFilter -RemotePort 22 -SettingName "Priority" -SettingValue "High".

Get-NetTCPSetting and Set-NetTCPSetting

These cmdlets allow you to view and modify the TCP settings, which can be crucial for optimizing performance for specific applications.

For example, to change the TCP receive window size, you can use Set-NetTCPSetting -SettingName "Custom" -TcpReceiveWindow 65536.

Test-Connection with -MtuSize and -Ttl

Although Test-Connection has already been mentioned, its -MtuSize and -Ttl parameters are worth learning for more advanced network diagnosis. These allow you to test the Maximum Transmission Unit (MTU) and Time To Live (TTL) for packets to a specific destination.

Invoke-Command with -Session

While not solely a network cmdlet, Invoke-Command can be used to execute commands on remote computers over the network. Using the -Session parameter, you can run a series of commands on a remote machine within a single session, making it very efficient for complex tasks.

Using these above advanced levels of cmdlets, PowerShell users can take their network management and troubleshooting to the next level to perform complex network operations that go far beyond basic connectivity checks.

System Monitoring

Monitoring a system is crucial in an IT environment, and PowerShell offers a variety of cmdlets designed specifically for this purpose. Effective system monitoring entails keeping track of metrics such as CPU usage, memory utilisation, disc activity, and network performance. Now, we shall explore some cmdlets that can assist in system monitoring as below:

Get-Process

Get-Process allows you to obtain a list of all the process running on your local or a remote machine. This cmdlet can be useful for checking CPU and memory utilization for each process.

Get-Process -Name explorer

This command fetches details about the 'explorer' process, including its CPU and memory utilization.

Get-Service

Using Get-Service, you can monitor the status of services on your machine or on a remote machine. This cmdlet displays whether a service is running, stopped, or paused.

Get-Service -Name wuauserv

This command will show the status of the Windows Update service (wuauserv).

Get-EventLog

Get-EventLog cmdlet allows you to query entries from the event log, offering insights into system activities and potential issues.

Get-EventLog -LogName System -Newest 10

The command above fetches the 10 most recent entries from the System event log.

Get-Counter

Get-Counter is used for capturing performance counter data. Performance counters provide various metrics about system performance.

Get-Counter -Counter "\Processor(_Total)\% Processor Time" -SampleInterval 2 -MaxSamples 3

The command Get-Counter -Counter "\Processor(_Total)\% Processor Time" -SampleInterval 2 -MaxSamples 3 monitors the total CPU usage at 2-second intervals, collecting three samples to track CPU performance over time.

Get-WmiObject

WMI (Windows Management Instrumentation) is a powerful feature. The Get-WmiObject cmdlet can fetch a treasure trove of system information. For instance, to get the amount of free disk space on your system:

Get-WmiObject -Class Win32_LogicalDisk -Filter "DeviceID='C:'" | Select-Object FreeSpace

Test-Connection for Continuous Ping

While we learned Test-Connection in the previous section under network-related cmdlets, it also serves as a monitoring tool when you need to continuously check the network status to a specific server.

Test-Connection -ComputerName google.com -Count 20

This command pings google.com 20 times and can be considered as a rudimentary form of network monitoring.

Get-HotFix

The Get-HotFix cmdlet lets you determine which patches have been applied to the system, aiding in vulnerability management.

Get-HotFix -Description "Security Update"

This command lists all the security updates applied to the system.

Measure-Command

This cmdlet allows you to measure the time it takes to run script blocks, giving you a way to monitor script performance.

Measure-Command {Get-ChildItem C:\ -Recurse}

This command calculates the time it takes to list all items under the C:\ directory recursively.

Get-Disk

Get-Disk can fetch detailed information about disk drives, including types (SSD, HDD), statuses, and sizes, which is critical for storage monitoring.

```
Get-Disk | Where-Object MediaType -eq 'SSD'
```

This command fetches information about all SSDs on your system.

Get-NetAdapterStatistics

This cmdlet offers comprehensive network adapter statistics. By using Get-NetAdapterStatistics -Name "Ethernet", you can obtain detailed data about the "Ethernet" network adapter, such as bytes sent and received and packets sent and received, assisting in network performance analysis.

```
Get-NetAdapterStatistics -Name "Ethernet"
```

This command will get statistics for the "Ethernet" adapter, such as bytes sent and received, and packets sent and received.

These cmdlets provide the ability to monitor various system metrics, ensuring that you have the necessary tools to maintain a smoothly running environment. Using these tools allows for the monitoring of performance, identification of bottlenecks, and implementation of preventive measures to mitigate system failure.

Text Manipulation

Text manipulation is an essential skill, especially for those who handle configuration files, logs, or any text-based data. PowerShell offers an array of cmdlets for text manipulation tasks, allowing you to sift through, alter, or transform textual content.

Get-Content

The Get-Content cmdlet is used to read the contents of a file. It outputs the file content line by line by default.

```
Get-Content -Path C:\path\to\file.txt
```

When you execute Get-Content -Path C:\path\to\file.txt, it displays the content of file.txt in your

PowerShell console. It supports various encoding types and allows you to read specific numbers of lines from the start or end of a file.

Set-Content
Set-Content can set the content of a text file to the specified value.

Set-Content -Path C:\path\to\file.txt -Value "New content here."

The command Set-Content -Path C:\path\to\file.txt -Value "New content here." will overwrite file.txt with "New content here." It replaces the entire content of the file with the specified value and supports different encodings. Unlike Add-Content, it does not append but replaces the existing content.

Add-Content
Add-Content appends content to a text file, rather than overwriting it. This cmdlet is particularly useful for updating logs or configuration files without losing the existing data.

Add-Content -Path C:\path\to\file.txt -Value "Appended text."

This command appends "Appended text." to the existing content of file.txt.

Out-File
The Out-File cmdlet directs output into a text file, essentially letting you save the output of a command.

Get-Process | Out-File -FilePath C:\path\to\output.txt

This command saves the list of running processes to output.txt.

Select-String
Select-String allows you to search through strings or files for a particular pattern, much like 'grep' in Unix/Linux systems.

Select-String -Path C:\path\to\file.txt -Pattern "SearchText"

This will find lines containing "SearchText" in file.txt.

Replace Operator

PowerShell allows you to use the -replace operator to substitute text.

$myString = "I like cats."
$newString = $myString -replace "cats", "dogs"

The value of $newString would be "I like dogs."

-split and -join Operators

The -split operator splits a string into an array based on a delimiter, and -join does the opposite.

$splitString = "apple,orange,banana" -split ","
$joinString = $splitString -join ";"

$splitString will be an array ("apple", "orange", "banana"), and $joinString will be "apple;orange;banana".

ConvertTo-Json and ConvertFrom-Json

These cmdlets allow you to convert objects to and from JSON format, which is useful when working with APIs.

$myObject = @{
  name = "John"
  age = 30
}
$jsonObject = $myObject | ConvertTo-Json

Here, $jsonObject will contain the JSON representation of $myObject.

Format-Table and Format-List

These cmdlets allow you to format output into a table or list format, improving readability.

Get-Process | Format-Table -Property Name, CPU

This command will display the process names and their respective CPU utilization in a table format.

Sort-Object

This cmdlet sorts objects based on property values, and it can be valuable when you have to arrange data.

Get-Process | Sort-Object -Property CPU -Descending

This command sorts processes based on CPU usage in descending order.

By becoming proficient in these cmdlets and operators, you gain access to potent tools for manipulating text. These utilities allow you to create scripts for a wide range of tasks, ranging from basic text replacements to intricate data parsing operations. Having a solid grasp of text manipulation in PowerShell allows you to efficiently handle tasks such as configuration management, log analysis, and data transformation.

Popular Flags and Parameters

Flags and parameters are crucial elements for enhancing the functionality and versatility of PowerShell cmdlets. They provide fine-grained control over the actions a cmdlet performs. We shall explore some commonly used flags and parameters, and understand their usage context.

-Verbose

The -Verbose flag is used to produce detailed information about the operation being performed. For example, using New-Item to create a new folder can be accompanied by -Verbose for more detailed output.

New-Item -Path "C:\NewFolder" -ItemType Directory -Verbose

-Force

The -Force flag is employed when you want to override protection mechanisms, or when you wish to avoid confirmation prompts. Be cautious; using -Force can overwrite data.

Remove-Item -Path "C:\SomeFolder" -Force

-Recurse

The -Recurse flag is often used with file and directory-related cmdlets to include all subdirectories or nested items.

Get-ChildItem -Path "C:\SomeFolder" -Recurse

-WhatIf
The -WhatIf flag is a "dry-run" flag, allowing you to see what a cmdlet would do without actually making changes. This is valuable for testing.

Remove-Item -Path "C:\SomeFolder" -WhatIf

-Credential
The -Credential parameter allows you to specify alternate credentials when executing a cmdlet. This is essential when executing commands on a remote server or for accounts with special permissions.

Get-WmiObject -Class Win32_BIOS -ComputerName RemotePC -Credential (Get-Credential)

-Filter
The -Filter parameter helps you narrow down the output of a cmdlet by applying criteria. It is more efficient than piping the output to Where-Object.

Get-ChildItem -Path "C:\SomeFolder" -Filter "*.txt"

-OutputFormat
This parameter is used to specify the output format. For example, Get-Process can have its output set to XML for easier parsing later.

Get-Process -OutputFormat XML

-Property
The -Property parameter lets you specify which properties of an object you want to retrieve or manipulate. This is used extensively in cmdlets like Select-Object and Sort-Object.

Get-Process | Sort-Object -Property CPU

-AsJob
The -AsJob parameter allows you to run a cmdlet as a background job, particularly useful for long-running tasks.

Test-Connection -ComputerName RemotePC -AsJob

-Include and -Exclude
These parameters allow you to include or exclude specific items in a cmdlet operation. These are generally used with file and folder manipulation cmdlets.

Get-ChildItem -Path "C:\SomeFolder" -Include "*.txt" -Exclude "example.txt"

-ErrorAction
The -ErrorAction parameter helps you define what to do when a cmdlet encounters an error. Options include Stop, Continue, SilentlyContinue, and Inquire.

Get-Content -Path "C:\invalidPath" -ErrorAction SilentlyContinue

The behaviour of cmdlets in PowerShell can be greatly influenced by the use of flags and parameters. You have the flexibility to customise commands to suit your specific requirements, such as sorting objects, executing tasks quietly, or utilising different credentials. These options enhance your PowerShell experience by providing you with precise control over operations, resulting in scripts that are more robust, modular, and efficient.

Inbuilt Alias and Shortcuts

Aliases and shortcuts are essential in PowerShell as they enhance efficiency by minimizing the need for extensive typing when executing commands. They serve as shorter, frequently shortened names for cmdlets and functions. We shall take a look at how to understand, discover, and apply these time-saving features.

Understanding Aliases
Aliases are alternative names for cmdlets and are created for convenience. For example, the cmdlet

Get-Command has an alias gcm. You can use either to execute the command.

```
Get-Command
```

Or using the alias:

```
gcm
```

Discovering Aliases

PowerShell has a cmdlet to help you list all the existing aliases, Get-Alias.

```
Get-Alias
```

This will return a list of all aliases available in your session, along with the cmdlets they map to. To find an alias for a particular cmdlet, you can use the -Definition parameter.

```
Get-Alias -Definition Get-Command
```

Common Aliases

Following are some commonly used aliases:

- ls and dir for Get-ChildItem
- cd for Set-Location
- cp for Copy-Item
- mv for Move-Item
- rm for Remove-Item
- ps for Get-Process
- kill for Stop-Process
- man for Get-Help

- echo for Write-Output
- cat for Get-Content

Creating Custom Aliases

You can create your own aliases using the Set-Alias cmdlet.

Set-Alias -Name "nf" -Value New-Item

This creates an alias nf for the New-Item cmdlet. Note that custom aliases are not persistent; they are only available for the current session.

Exporting and Importing Aliases

If you wish to keep your custom aliases across sessions, you can export them into a file and then import them when needed.

Get-Alias | Export-Csv -Path "C:\alias_list.csv"

And to import:

Import-Csv -Path "C:\alias_list.csv" | ForEach-Object { Set-Alias -Name $_.Name -Value $_.Definition }

Shortcuts in the Pipeline

Pipelines (|) allow you to pass the output of one cmdlet as input to another. While not aliases per se, they function as shortcuts for extended operations. For example:

Get-Process | Where-Object { $_.CPU -gt 10 }

Here, Where-Object is often aliased as where, making the command shorter and quicker to type.

Function Keys

Function keys serve as handy shortcuts:

- F7: Brings up a command history menu

- F8: Autocomplete from command history

- F9: Allows you to type a number to execute a command from the history list

- Shift+F10: Shows the context menu

Special Characters

PowerShell uses special characters for shortcuts in operations.

Some commonly used ones are:

- $_: Current object in the pipeline

- %: Alias for ForEach-Object

- ?: Alias for Where-Object

- !!: Execute the last command

Using aliases and shortcuts can improve the efficiency of your PowerShell experience by minimizing keystrokes. By employing different techniques like using aliases, creating custom ones, incorporating special characters, and utilizing function keys, these features enable you to allocate more time and attention to the current task.

Summary

The chapter extensively examined the usefulness and effectiveness of aliases and shortcuts in PowerShell. Starting with an explanation of aliases, it was discovered that they function as alternative names, typically shortened, for cmdlets. By implementing these methods, one can greatly decrease the need for excessive typing, resulting in improved productivity. Cmdlets such as Get-Alias can be utilized to find aliases that already exist, while the Set-Alias cmdlet enables the creation of custom aliases. The custom aliases learned are specific to each session, but we also covered techniques for exporting and importing them to verify that they can be used in future sessions.

In the chapter, the author taught common aliases in PowerShell, including ls, cd, and rm, which are frequently encountered by most users. Aliases in PowerShell often resemble commands found in other shell environments, which can facilitate the transition for individuals who are already familiar with UNIX-like systems. These aliases have various purposes, including file operations, system monitoring, and text manipulation. In addition, the option to create custom aliases allows users to customize their PowerShell environment to suit their individual requirements and workflow.

Pipelines and special characters were introduced as additional methods to streamline intricate operations. The pipeline allows for smooth data flow between cmdlets, effectively reducing code complexity. Special characters such as $_ for the current object in the pipeline and % as an alias for ForEach-Object enhance the scripting process. Using these unique characters not only reduces the length of the script, but also enhances its readability and manageability.

Additional tools were introduced to enhance task efficiency, such as function keys like F7 for command history and F8 for autocomplete. These keys provide efficient methods for revisiting or executing commands, thereby reducing the need to repeatedly type the same or similar commands. By utilizing aliases, shortcuts, and function keys, users can enhance their navigation of PowerShell, enabling them to concentrate on problem-solving rather than syntax.

Chapter 3: Working with PowerShell ISE

PowerShell ISE Overview

In this chapter, you will be introduced to the PowerShell Integrated Scripting Environment (ISE), which is a crucial tool in the PowerShell ecosystem. This chapter will provide you with a practical understanding of how to use the ISE effectively. PowerShell ISE is a powerful tool that makes script development and testing easier. It provides a variety of features to streamline the scripting process. You have the freedom to personalize the graphical interface to your liking, with a wide range of layouts and themes available for you to choose from. ISE offers a solid range of features from the start, but its true strength lies in its ability to be customized and expanded. You have the ability to enhance its capabilities by incorporating modules and add-ons, allowing you to tailor it to your specific requirements.

The interface of PowerShell ISE is designed to be user-friendly and easy to navigate. The interface is organized into different panes, such as the Script Pane, Console Pane, and Output Pane, each with its own unique function. Users can easily customize the interface by dragging and dropping elements, making it more user-friendly and personalized. If you're looking for a dark theme to enhance your coding experience during long hours, or if you want to rearrange panes for better screen utilization, PowerShell ISE is the perfect solution for you.

PowerShell ISE excels in the field of debugging. You can easily debug your code using the built-in tools. These tools allow you to set breakpoints, step into functions, and inspect variable values while your code is running. This is especially helpful for pinpointing any issues with logic or performance in your scripts. The inclusion of an integrated debugger enhances code execution by providing a step-by-step analysis, enabling a deeper comprehension of the code's progression and simplifying the debugging procedure. In addition, you have the ability to view and stop running scripts, giving you control and visibility over script execution.

In this chapter, we will cover the most effective ways to utilize PowerShell ISE. Knowing how to write, format, and save scripts properly can help you avoid hours of troubleshooting later on. In addition, understanding how to efficiently utilize the built-in cmdlet and function libraries can help you save time and produce cleaner code. For instance, incorporating ISE snippets can assist you in swiftly inserting frequently-used sections of code. These best practices help ensure smoother development cycles by providing guidelines for effective debugging, code commenting, and keyboard shortcuts.

Finally, we will also cover various ways to enhance the capabilities of PowerShell ISE. Enhance your ISE experience with a range of modules and add-ons. We offer a variety of tools, including advanced debugging tools and modules for code refactoring. When it comes to refactoring, being able to restructure code without changing how it works on the outside is crucial for making it easier to maintain. ISE add-ons offer automation for code refactoring, enhancing code efficiency and readability with minimal manual effort.

Our goal is to help you become skilled in using PowerShell ISE by covering a range of topics including interface customization, debugging techniques, best practices, and extending the functionality of PowerShell ISE.

ISE Interface and Components

The PowerShell Integrated Scripting Environment (ISE) provides a user-friendly graphical interface that greatly improves the overall experience of using PowerShell. The interface of ISE is designed with different panes and toolbars that enhance the scripting, testing, and debugging process.

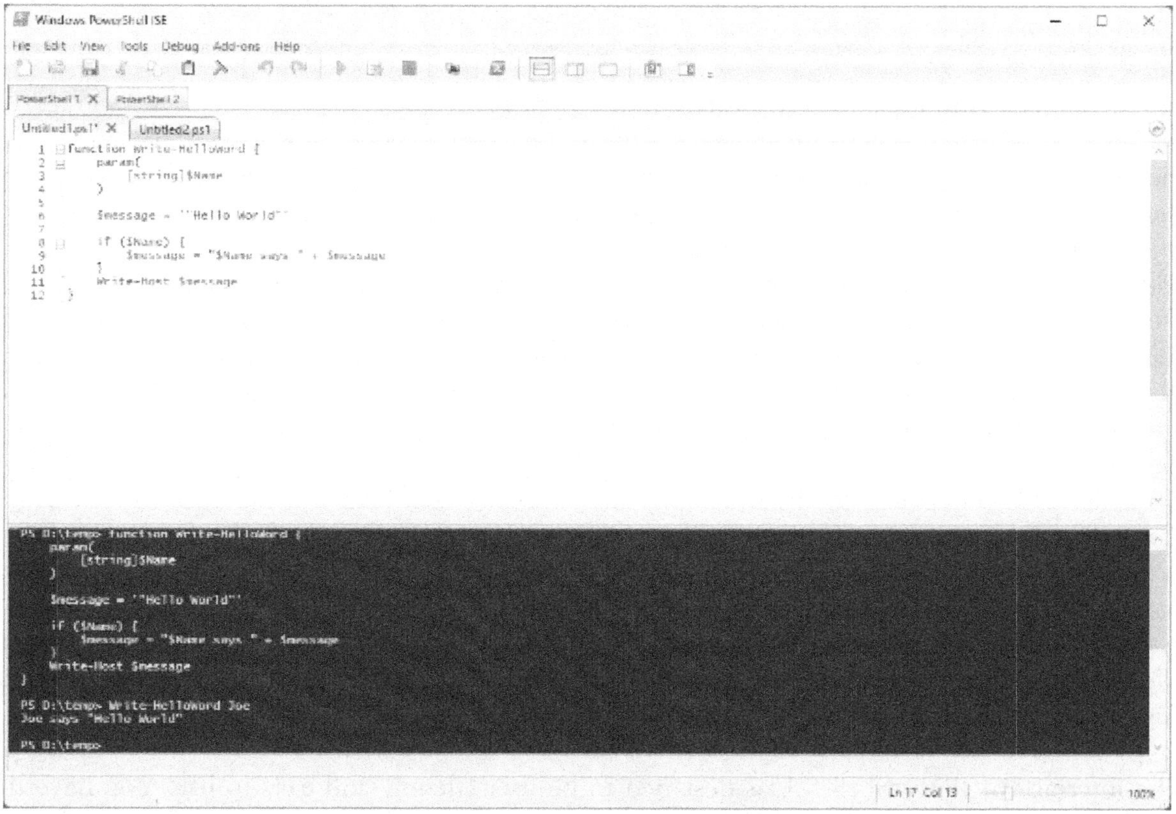

Fig 3.1 PowerShell ISE Interface

First, we should learn about the Script Pane, which is considered the central component of PowerShell ISE. This is the place for writing your scripts or commands. The Script Pane has syntax highlighting, which helps you differentiate between cmdlets, variables, and parameters. This makes it easier to work with and understand your code. You have the option to open multiple script tabs, with each one functioning as its own separate instance of the Script Pane. This is particularly useful when you have to work on multiple scripts at the same time or need to refer back and forth between scripts.

Now, we shall move on to the Console Pane. This section is typically located below the Script Pane and allows you to execute individual PowerShell commands. The Script Pane is used for developing and editing scripts, while the Console Pane is designed for quickly executing commands. You can run any command from the PowerShell console here, and see the results in the Output Pane next to it. You have the option to switch between multi-line and single-line modes, giving you the flexibility to adapt to your specific requirements. Next to the Console Pane, you'll find the Output Pane. This pane shows the results of your commands or scripts. Customize the color schemes for the Output Pane to easily distinguish between different types of outputs. Furthermore, by simply clicking on any object in the Output Pane, you can easily access more information, such as property details. This feature proves helpful for troubleshooting or analyzing your code's results.

The Command Add-on is usually located on the right-hand side. This is a user-friendly graphical interface that displays a comprehensive list of all the cmdlets, functions, workflows, and aliases installed on your system. By selecting any of these options, you will find a short description and the syntax, allowing you to easily insert them into your script. This is especially helpful for individuals who might not recall every cmdlet or are new to PowerShell scripting. Another useful add-on is the Snippets Add-on, which works in conjunction with the Command Add-on. Snippets are ready-made code segments that can be easily inserted into your script. They are really useful for automating the inclusion of repetitive code segments. To access them, simply click on the desired snippet and insert it at the current cursor position in the Script Pane. You can also customize and save snippets, creating a library of code that can be reused.

To assist with debugging, the interface provides a Debug Toolbar. On this toolbar, you'll find icons that allow you to set breakpoints, step into and over commands, and stop the debugger. When debugging, you have the option to inspect variables in the Output Pane or execute commands in the Immediate Pane without impacting the running script. At last, the Menu Bar and the Toolbar provide a variety of options and functions. These toolbars simplify navigation, allowing you to easily save, open, run, and stop files and scripts. You can access options to customize the ISE environment, like changing fonts or colors, from this menu.

The interface of PowerShell ISE is designed to be user-friendly and easy to use. You have the flexibility to resize and rearrange the panes based on your preferences. You have the freedom to personalize the workspace to your liking, allowing PowerShell ISE to become a versatile tool that caters to your specific requirements. By grasping the role of each interface component, you can enhance your efficiency and productivity when scripting in PowerShell.

ISE Customization

Getting the PowerShell ISE interface customized is a must if you want to streamline your processes, match the tool to your requirements, and create a more efficient and individualized scripting environment. You have the ability to make various adjustments to the interface, including visual elements such as themes and fonts, as well as the layout of different panes.

Visual Elements

The first step to customize the appearance usually involves modifying the theme. The default theme may not be the most eye-friendly for prolonged periods, and ISE allows you to change it. To set a new theme, navigate to Tools > Options. Under the General Settings tab, you will find a Color Theme dropdown where you can select from pre-built themes.

You can also alter the fonts and colors used within the Script Pane, Console Pane, and Output Pane. Under Tools > Options, select the Fonts and Colors tab. From here, you can tweak the fonts, background color, text color, etc., to your liking.

Layout Customization

The layout of PowerShell ISE is incredibly flexible. You can rearrange panes, dock or undock them, and adjust their sizes. The mouse and the drag-and-drop feature are your best friends here. You can drag the title bar of any pane to move it around or hover over the edge of a pane until the cursor changes to a resizing icon, and then drag to resize.

Tabs and Files

PowerShell ISE allows you to work on multiple files simultaneously through the use of tabs. You can configure settings related to tabs through the Tools > Options menu under the General Settings tab. Here, you can choose to open new tabs for each new script or set tabs to auto-save.

Custom Profiles and Functions

PowerShell ISE enables you to write a profile script that runs every time the ISE starts. In this script, you can include functions, aliases, or any other code you want to be available every time you open ISE. The profile script is located in your home directory and is named Microsoft.PowerShellISE_profile.ps1. To create or edit this file, run $profile in the Console Pane to display the path, and then use the notepad command to open it.

In the profile script, you can add code to further customize ISE. For example, you might include functions that set up your workspace exactly how you like it. Once you've edited the profile script, save the changes and restart the ISE to see them take effect.

Adding Custom Menu Items

For advanced users, you can extend the functionality of the Menu Bar by adding custom menu items that execute specific scripts. To add a new menu item, you would use the Add-ons menu. Under Tools > Add-ons, you can add, manage, and remove these custom functionalities. The process involves creating a PowerShell script that contains the functionality you want and then registering that script as an add-on within ISE.

Debug Toolbar

The Debug Toolbar can be customized to include buttons for specific debug actions that you use frequently. Go to View > Show Toolbar to ensure the toolbar is visible, then right-click on it to select Customize. From here, you can add, remove, or rearrange buttons.

Creating Custom Key Bindings

Finally, PowerShell ISE allows you to modify or add keyboard shortcuts for almost any action. Navigate to Tools > Options and under the General Settings tab, you'll find an option to manage key bindings.

One of the most powerful features of PowerShell ISE is its ability to customize the environment to suit your needs. These alterations, which range from aesthetic adjustments to functional adjustments, can greatly improve your programming experience.

ISE for Performance and Productivity

For maximum efficiency and productivity, you should customize the PowerShell ISE interface if you are spending a lot of time in scripting. Although we have covered the interface customization option in the previous section, we still can explore another most effective approach(es) to get the ideal configuration for your particular requirements.

"Layering" Approach

One effective approach is to layer your customization starting from the most basic to the most complex changes. This enables you to build upon the base settings and adapt as you become more comfortable with the environment.

Layer 1: Aesthetic Foundation

Start by setting a comfortable theme, fonts, and colors. This sets the aesthetic foundation for your workspace. For this, it's essential to think long-term; choose a theme and font that are eye-friendly and conducive to extended periods of work. You can set these in Tools > Options under the Fonts and Colors tab.

Layer 2: Layout Streamlining
After aesthetics, focus on optimizing the layout. Begin by identifying the panes and features you use most frequently. Once identified, you can relocate these panes for easier access, either through dragging their title bars or through the View menu. For example, if you frequently switch between the Console Pane and the Output Pane, consider arranging them adjacent to each other.

Layer 3: Custom Profiles for Task Automation
For those who use PowerShell ISE for specific, repetitive tasks, a custom profile script is invaluable. A profile script in ISE can contain functions, modules, and even GUI adjustments that apply every time you start the ISE. You could have a profile script that auto-loads certain modules or sets the ISE window size to your preferred dimensions.

To start building a profile script, navigate to the Console Pane and type $profile. This will return the location where your profile script should be stored. Use a text editor to create or modify this script with the custom functions you want.

Layer 4: Toolbar and Shortcut Key Customization
This is often considered an advanced layer. Once you're comfortable with PowerShell ISE, the next step is to adapt the toolbar and keyboard shortcuts to align with your specific workflow. You can customize the Debug Toolbar by going to View > Show Toolbar and then right-clicking to select Customize. Keyboard shortcuts can be set under Tools > Options in the General Settings tab.

Layer 5: Extending with Add-ons
The final layer involves adding custom menu items and additional functionalities via add-ons. The add-on feature is quite powerful and allows you to add custom scripts to the menu bar. Under Tools > Add-ons, you can manage and even create your own add-ons. This enables you to integrate third-party tools or custom scripts seamlessly into your ISE environment.

Iterative, Shared and Team Customization

Another important factor to consider is the process of making adjustments and improvements over time. As you become more familiar with PowerShell ISE, your requirements might evolve. Do not forget to regularly check and update your customization settings. Take, for example, a tool that used to be essential but now it's no longer needed, or you might discover better ways to get a task done. Flexibility is crucial.

Standardizing certain customizations across a team can be advantageous in an enterprise environment. This helps create a reliable environment, facilitating smoother collaboration. Nevertheless, finding a middle ground between uniformity and individual tastes is crucial. Team members can start with a set of shared customizations and then personalize them to fit their needs.

By following this methodical approach, you can create a scripting environment that is optimized, efficient, and personalized to your needs.

Script Debugging

Debugging is a cornerstone skill for anyone who works with PowerShell ISE, especially as your scripts become more complex and involved. We shall consider a use case where you've written a script to move files older than 30 days from one directory to another but are experiencing issues with its performance or output. How do you go about debugging this?

Debugging Environment in ISE

Firstly, familiarize yourself with the debugging environment in PowerShell ISE. You have options to set breakpoints, step into functions, step over lines of code, and observe variable values. These can be accessed from the Debug menu or by using their respective shortcut keys. For instance, F9 sets or removes a breakpoint, F10 steps over a line, and F11 steps into a function.

Setting Breakpoints

In your script, set a breakpoint at a strategic location to start your debugging. Let us assume the breakpoint is at the line that calls the function to move files. In ISE, you can either click on the left-hand side of the script pane beside the line number or press F9 while the line is selected. A red dot will appear, indicating that a breakpoint is set.

```
# Sample code snippet
$sourceFolder = "C:\Source"
$destFolder = "C:\Destination"
$files = Get-ChildItem -Path $sourceFolder

# Set breakpoint here
foreach ($file in $files) {
    # More code here
}
```

Stepping through Code

Once the breakpoint is set, run your script by clicking the 'Run Script' button or pressing F5. The script execution will stop at the breakpoint. Here, you can either:

Step Into (F11)
If the line contains a function or script block, using this option will step into that specific piece of code.

Step Over (F10)
This allows you to execute the current line and stop at the next one.

Continue (F5)
This continues the script execution until it hits another breakpoint or finishes.

Observing Variables

In our considered environment, it would be wise to observe the $files variable to ensure it contains the correct data. When you hit a breakpoint, the variables pane will show you the current value of all variables in scope. You can also hover your mouse over a variable in the script pane to see its current value.

Using Console Pane

The Console Pane is particularly useful when debugging. While the script is paused, you can execute commands in the Console Pane to change variable values, invoke functions, or even run scripts. This can be beneficial for quickly testing a piece of code or command without having to stop debugging, modify the script, and start over.

```
# Example in Console Pane
$files.Count  # This will return the number of files to be moved
```

If your script calls external functions or modules, you can also step into these when debugging. This is particularly useful if you suspect the issue might be within an external function rather than your main script.

Advanced Breakpoints

PowerShell ISE allows for advanced breakpoints like conditional breakpoints or breakpoints that trigger on variable value changes. For example, you could set a breakpoint to trigger only when a variable reaches a particular value.

```
# Command to set a conditional breakpoint
Set-PSBreakpoint -Variable files -Mode Read -Action {if ($files.Count -lt 1) {break}}
```

This advanced feature allows for targeted debugging, saving you time and effort as you sift through your script.

Script Output and Logs

Lastly, don't ignore the script output pane and any logs you may have implemented. These can provide crucial clues on where things are going wrong or why a particular operation failed.

PowerShell ISE Add-Ons

One of the underappreciated strengths of PowerShell ISE is its extensibility. By using add-ons, you can tailor your development environment to better suit your workflow, incorporate new functionalities, or even automate repetitive tasks. Extending PowerShell ISE functionality through add-ons can transform your coding experience. We shall dive into this by considering a practical use case: You wish to add a custom menu to PowerShell ISE that would allow you to insert predefined code snippets.

Before you can start creating add-ons, you need to understand the $psISE object which will be explained in detail in the next section. This object is the gateway to customizing PowerShell ISE, as it exposes various methods and properties that enable you to manipulate the ISE environment. This object has various properties like CurrentPowerShellTab, Options, and CustomMenus, among others, which you will leverage to create your add-on.

Your First Add-On

Let us create a custom menu that lets you insert a 'Hello, World!' script or a script template for error handling. This will involve the following steps:

Create a Custom Menu
First, initialize a new menu item and define its text label.

```
$customMenu = $psISE.CurrentPowerShellTab.AddOnsMenu.Submenus.Add("Custom Snippets", [scriptblock]::Create(''), $null)
```

Add Sub-Menus
Now we shall add the specific code snippets as sub-menus to this custom menu.

```
$helloWorldSnippet = {
    $psISE.CurrentFile.Editor.InsertText("Write-Host 'Hello, World!'")
}
$customMenu.Submenus.Add("Insert 'Hello, World!'",
[scriptblock]::Create($helloWorldSnippet), 'Ctrl+Alt+H')


$errorHandlingSnippet = {
    $snippetText = @"
try {
    # Code
}
catch {
    Write-Host $_.Exception.Message
}
"@
    $psISE.CurrentFile.Editor.InsertText($snippetText)
}
$customMenu.Submenus.Add("Insert Error Handling Template",
[scriptblock]::Create($errorHandlingSnippet), 'Ctrl+Alt+E')
```

Add Keyboard Shortcuts
The above examples also include keyboard shortcuts (Ctrl+Alt+H and Ctrl+Alt+E) for quick access to these snippets.

Test Your Add-On
To test, you need to execute the script that contains these commands. Post-execution, your custom menu should appear in the Add-ons menu of PowerShell ISE. Selecting the respective options should insert the snippets into your current file.

Advanced Customizations
Dynamic Menus
Suppose you want your menu to be populated dynamically based on some condition. In that case,

you can use a ScriptBlock to populate the menu dynamically.

```
$dynamicMenuScript = {
    $menu = $psISE.CurrentPowerShellTab.AddOnsMenu.Submenus | Where-Object { $_.DisplayName -eq "Dynamic Snippets" }
    $menu.Submenus.Clear()

    $snippets = Get-Content "C:\Path\To\DynamicSnippets.txt"  # Assuming one snippet per line
    foreach ($snippet in $snippets) {
        $menu.Submenus.Add("Insert $snippet", [scriptblock]::Create("`$psISE.CurrentFile.Editor.InsertText('$snippet')"), $null)
    }
}
$psISE.CurrentPowerShellTab.AddOnsMenu.Submenus.Add("Dynamic Snippets", [scriptblock]::Create($dynamicMenuScript), $null)
```

Integrating External Tools

You can also integrate external tools and scripts into your ISE session. For instance, you could add a Git commit option that triggers a commit for the current script.

```
$gitCommit = {
    Set-Location $psISE.CurrentFile.FullPath | Split-Path
    git add .
    git commit -m "Committed through ISE"
}
$psISE.CurrentPowerShellTab.AddOnsMenu.Submenus.Add("Git Commit", [scriptblock]::Create($gitCommit), 'Ctrl+Alt+G')
```

If you have a library of custom functions, consider adding them to your profile script ($PROFILE) so that they autoload when you start ISE. This way, they can be readily available for use in your add-ons. With the capability to add menus, integrate external tools, and even populate menus dynamically, extending PowerShell ISE through add-ons empowers you to create a customized, efficient, and powerful development environment.

PowerShell ISE Object Model

In the PowerShell Integrated Scripting Environment (ISE), the $psISE object is a goldmine for automation and customization. It provides a series of properties and methods that you can manipulate to change various aspects of the ISE's behavior. So far, you've seen how to create add-ons, but we shall delve deeper into the unique functionalities that $psISE enables, such as handling files, tabs, and options. We will continue with a use-case where you want to build an intelligent session manager for your PowerShell ISE.

Managing Files

You can open files in ISE by utilizing the CurrentPowerShellTab property.

$filePath = "C:\Path\To\Your\File.ps1"
$psISE.CurrentPowerShellTab.Files.Add($filePath)

You can also save the current file using $psISE.

$psISE.CurrentFile.Save()

You might want to save the current script with a different name.

$newFilePath = "C:\Path\To\New\File.ps1"
$psISE.CurrentFile.SaveAs($newFilePath)

Managing Tabs

If you're working on multiple scripts, you can create a new tab easily.

$psISE.PowerShellTabs.Add()

This might require a bit of PowerShell scripting, but it's doable. You can enumerate the available tabs and then activate the one you want.

$allTabs = $psISE.PowerShellTabs
$allTabs[1].Activate()

Manipulating Options

Tired of squinting at your code? You can adjust the font size for better readability.

$psISE.Options.FontSize = 14

If you wish to change the background color of the scripting pane, you can.

$psISE.Options.ScriptPaneBackgroundColor = 'White'

Session Management

Imagine you have a bunch of script files that you always work on together. Wouldn't it be nice to open them all at once, each in its tab? The $psISE object can help you automate this.

You can create a script that opens specific files each in a new tab. This is particularly useful if you're working on a large project with multiple related files.

$filePaths = @("C:\Path\To\File1.ps1", "C:\Path\To\File2.ps1")
foreach ($path in $filePaths) {
   $newTab = $psISE.PowerShellTabs.Add()
   $newTab.Files.Add($path)
}

If you want this setup to load every time you start PowerShell ISE, you can add the script to your ISE profile ($profile), which runs every time ISE starts.

You can create a snapshot of your current session (tabs and files open) and save it as a script. This script, when run, will restore your ISE environment to the snapshot state.

$snapshotScript = "C:\Path\To\SessionSnapshot.ps1"
$currentFiles = $psISE.PowerShellTabs | ForEach-Object { $_.Files } | Select-Object -

and commits (git commit) the changes.

Using Git

Git integration allows you to easily manage different versions of your scripts. If a script encounters issues as a result of modifications, you have the option to effortlessly revert back to a previous stable version.

With PowerShell ISE, you have the ability to clone repositories and immediately begin contributing to collaborative projects. Performing Git operations alongside code edits makes code reviews and merges much more efficient.

With Git, you have the option to create branches for working on separate features or bugs. ISE allows you to easily create, switch, and merge branches, streamlining your workflow.

Git commits include a timestamp and the author's information. This tool is great for auditing changes, which is particularly helpful in regulated environments.

You can commit specific parts of your changes using Git's staging area. In the ISE console, you have the option to manually run git add to stage specific changes. This allows you to review the changes before committing them.

When collaborating with others, it's common to encounter merge conflicts. With Git integrated into ISE, you can quickly resolve conflicts right from the editor, saving you time and effort.

Experienced users have the option to enhance the automation of Git operations by creating scripts that can be triggered by specific events, such as saving a file or closing a tab. Utilizing the complete functionality of the $psISE object model.

You are adding the complete capabilities of source control management to your scripting environment by combining Git with PowerShell ISE. PowerShell scripting is moving closer to being in line with DevOps, and thus paves the way for more sophisticated techniques like Continuous Integration/Continuous Deployment (CI/CD).

Custom GUI Extensions

Custom GUIs enable you to add buttons, panels, and even custom dialogs to the existing ISE interface, empowering you with tools that automate repetitive tasks or simplify complex ones. For this exercise, we shall assume you want to create a custom panel that offers quick access to commonly used Git commands such as 'Commit', 'Push', and 'Pull'.

Before diving into the code, ensure you have the Windows Presentation Foundation (WPF) libraries loaded in your PowerShell ISE. If they're not, import them with:

Add-Type -AssemblyName PresentationFramework

Creating WPF Panel
Initialize XAML Markup
Define the XAML markup for your custom panel. This will specify the layout of the buttons, text fields, or any other GUI components.

```
$xaml = @"
<Grid>
   <Button Name="gitCommit" Content="Commit" Width="100" Height="30" VerticalAlignment="Top" HorizontalAlignment="Left"/>
   <Button Name="gitPush" Content="Push" Width="100" Height="30" VerticalAlignment="Top" HorizontalAlignment="Right"/>
   <Button Name="gitPull" Content="Pull" Width="100" Height="30" VerticalAlignment="Bottom" HorizontalAlignment="Left"/>
</Grid>
"@
```

Load XAML into WPF Object
Create a WPF object that will hold your XAML layout.

```
$reader = [System.Xml.XmlNodeReader]::new([System.Xml.Xml]::XmlDocument.LoadXml($xaml))
$gitPanel = [Windows.Markup.XamlReader]::Load($reader)
```

Add Event Handlers
Attach events like clicks to your buttons.

```
$gitPanel.gitCommit.Add_Click({Invoke-Expression "git commit -m 'Quick Commit'"})
```

$gitPanel.gitPush.Add_Click({Invoke-Expression "git push"})

$gitPanel.gitPull.Add_Click({Invoke-Expression "git pull"})

Embedding WPF Panel into ISE

To get this panel into the ISE, you can leverage the $psISE object model.

Create a Custom Tab

Start by adding a custom tab to ISE where your panel will reside.

$customTab = $psISE.CustomTabs.Add("Git Operations", $true)

Embed the Panel

Now add the WPF panel into this tab.

$customTab.Controls.Add($gitPanel)

For those who find Git's CLI intimidating or cumbersome, these buttons make version control accessible, allowing a broader team to contribute to projects. With just a click, you can commit changes, push to repositories, and pull updates. You can extend this example to add other buttons that perform tasks like stash, merge, or even revert commits.

Advanced users could integrate this with CI/CD pipelines. For instance, clicking the 'Push' button could automatically run tests before pushing to ensure code quality. You could create panels that take inputs through dropdowns, sliders, or checkboxes and dynamically run scripts based on these inputs.

Code Refactoring

Refactoring code involves enhancing the internal structure of a codebase while keeping its external behavior intact. The goal is to improve the code's efficiency, readability, and maintainability. Although your original script may be effective for its intended use, refactoring it will allow for scalability and adaptability, ultimately increasing its lifespan. Clean code is essential for long-term success in the fast-paced field of DevOps, where PowerShell is a go-to tool. It enables effortless debugging, simplified testing, and straightforward feature enhancements.

Importance

Readability: Well-structured code is easier to read and understand. This aids in quicker debugging and easier implementation of new features.

Maintainability: A well-organized codebase is simpler to maintain. New developers can easily understand and contribute to the project.

Performance: Refactoring can improve the performance by optimizing algorithms and eliminating redundant code, thereby using resources more efficiently.

Collaboration: In a team setting, readability and maintainability are vital. With everyone using the same coding standards, the team can collaborate more effectively.

Reduced Technical Debt: Every codebase accumulates technical debt over time. Refactoring helps in paying off this debt before it becomes unmanageable.

Sample Program: Refactoring Code in ISE

The script we will examine is a sample that transfers files across directories, determines their size, and records the data into a text document. We shall break down this example script into smaller, more manageable steps.

Suppose the original script looks something like this:

```
$source = "C:\SourceDir"
$dest = "C:\DestDir"
$files = Get-ChildItem -Path $source

foreach ($file in $files) {
    $filePath = $file.FullName
    $newPath = Join-Path -Path $dest -ChildPath $file.Name
    Copy-Item -Path $filePath  Destination $newPath
    $size = (Get-Item $newPath).length
    "$file copied and size is $size" | Out-File -FilePath "C:\log.txt" -Append
}
```

Breaking Down Functions

The first step is to break down the script into smaller, more manageable functions.

```
function Copy-Files($source, $dest) {
  # Code to copy files
}


function Log-FileDetails($filePath, $size) {
  # Code to log file details
}
```

Enhance Readability

Use descriptive variable names and include comments for better readability.

```
function Copy-Files($sourceDirectory, $destinationDirectory) {
  # Code to copy files
}


function Log-FileDetails($filePath, $fileSize) {
  # Code to log file details
}
```

Remove Redundancy

If any code is repeated, such as logging, move it to a separate function.

```
function Log-Action($message) {
  $message | Out-File -FilePath "C:\log.txt" -Append
}
```

Use Advanced Functions

PowerShell allows you to use advanced functions with parameters like [CmdletBinding()] and param().

```powershell
function Copy-Files {
  [CmdletBinding()]
  param(
    [Parameter(Mandatory=$true)]
    [string]$sourceDirectory,

    [Parameter(Mandatory=$true)]
    [string]$destinationDirectory
  )
  # Code to copy files
}
```

After completing this exercise, you will have improved the code's readability and maintainability. Additionally, you will have incorporated advanced features such as mandatory parameters and logging functions. Refactoring your code may initially appear to be a time-consuming task, but it ultimately proves to be beneficial in the long term, particularly as your codebase expands and develops. PowerShell ISE simplifies refactoring with its debugging and testing features, making coding best practices easier to implement.

Summary

This chapter explored the various features of PowerShell ISE, starting with an overview of its interface and how it works. Next, we moved on to personalizing the interface, honing in on ways to adjust it to meet specific needs. Through our research, we discovered methods for creating a user-friendly interface that caters to specific tasks. This includes the ability to personalize the Script pane and Console pane, as well as the convenience of saving and loading different layouts using profiles.

Next, we focused on the practical side of debugging. We discovered an example script that demonstrates how to copy files between directories. This script provides a practical approach to setting breakpoints, monitoring variables, and stepping through code to effectively identify any issues that may arise. Debugging plays a crucial role in coding, particularly in intricate scripts. It allows for quick identification and resolution of errors, leading to improved code quality.

We then delved into enhancing PowerShell ISE's capabilities, learning a range of advanced subjects. Some of the tasks involved were developing add-ons, using the $psISE object, incorporating Git for version control, and designing custom GUI extensions. The sections provided clear examples and use cases, highlighting the practical applications and advantages of these functionalities. The main emphasis was on how these extensions can assist in automating repetitive tasks, simplifying complex operations, and making the coding process more efficient.

Finally, we explored the world of code refactoring. We discovered how to efficiently modify code in PowerShell ISE without affecting its outward functionality. We implemented best practices such as improving readability, maintainability, and performance enhancement by breaking down a sample script into smaller, more manageable functions. We emphasized the significance of refactoring in coding, learning its importance in team environments and its ability to minimize technical debt. This in-depth examination of refactoring highlighted its usefulness as a continuous process that should be a fundamental aspect of every coding project.

Chapter 4: PowerShell Modules

Overview

In this chapter, we will explore one of PowerShell's powerful features, Modules. To begin, let us take a quick look at the many modules that make up the PowerShell ecosystem and highlight their functions as well as the versatility they offer when it comes to controlling Windows installations. Next, we will move on to the practical steps of installing and importing modules. You'll learn how to import and add pre-existing modules from various repositories into your sessions by taking advantage of PowerShell's command-line features.

Effective management is just as important as simply obtaining modules. We will now learn the most effective ways to manage modules. We will learn version control, dependency management, and guidelines to keep your modules secure, up-to-date, and reliable for deployment. Not only will this knowledge simplify your life, but it will also give you a strong foundation for upkeep of resilient IT systems.

Once we have a solid understanding of module management, we can move on to creating custom cmdlets. Through a real-world example, such as creating a custom cmdlet for managing Azure VMs, you can develop a thorough understanding of how to enhance PowerShell's functionality. This will enable you to build your own tools that are tailored to handle specific tasks effectively.

Lastly, we will cover error handling with cmdlets to wrap off this chapter. We will look at how PowerShell helps you catch and manage problems, giving you the precise information you need to troubleshoot without interfering needlessly with your processes. This is a feature that is sometimes disregarded but is essential for reliable, maintainable programming.

Modules in PowerShell

Modules are like self-contained packages that hold PowerShell components such as cmdlets, functions, variables, and workflows. They are designed to be reusable and easy to work with. They allow you to bundle a group of related functionalities, making distribution and usage more convenient. Modules are incredibly helpful in complex environments, where tasks are frequently repeated and can be automated.

Types of Modules

Script Modules
These are the most common types of modules and are basically .psm1 files that contain any valid PowerShell script code.

For instance, consider that you have a script for retrieving system logs. Instead of writing the same code repeatedly, you could package this as a script module.

Create a file named Get-SystemLog.psm1 and add the following function:

```
function Get-SystemLog {
    Get-EventLog -LogName System -Newest 20
}
```

To use this module, you'd simply import it:

```
Import-Module ./Get-SystemLog.psm1
```

Then, you can use the Get-SystemLog function as you normally would.

Binary Modules

These are written in languages like C# and compiled into a .dll file. They can implement functionalities that may not be achievable with simple script code. Binary modules can be more powerful and faster but require a language like C# for their creation. Assume you've created a .dll file that has a function to encrypt a string.

Firstly, you'd compile the C# code into a .dll file. Once done, you import the .dll into your PowerShell session:

```
Import-Module ./StringEncrypt.dll
```

After importing, you can use the cmdlets or functions defined in the .dll as if they were regular PowerShell cmdlets.

Manifest Modules

These are .psd1 files that serve as a module manifest. Manifest modules are created with a .psd1 extension and often accompany either script or binary modules to provide additional metadata. In other words, they act as the metadata for a module and define the characteristics and dependencies of the modules they represent.

For example, create a ModuleManifest.psd1 with something similar to:

```
@{
    ModuleVersion = '1.0'
```

```
    NestedModules = @('Get-SystemLog.psm1')
    FunctionsToExport = @('Get-SystemLog')
    PowerShellVersion = '5.1'
}
```

Importing the manifest module imports all nested modules and makes all defined functions available for use:

Import-Module ./ModuleManifest.psd1

The above sample program demonstrates how various modules can be constructed and applied using system logs, encryption, and metadata. If you're looking to handle local system logs, secure sensitive data, or distribute a set of related functionalities, modules provide a flexible and efficient solution for managing your PowerShell tasks.

Install Complex Modules

There are many different ways to install PowerShell modules, and installing sophisticated modules or ones not easily found in regular repositories can be especially difficult. It's important to have a good grasp of the details in order to successfully install these modules.

From PowerShell Gallery

The simplest way to install modules is from the PowerShell Gallery. Even some complex modules can be easily installed using this method. To install a module, you can run:

Install-Module -Name ModuleName

However, what if you need a specific version or want to install for all users? Parameters like -RequiredVersion or -Scope AllUsers become crucial:

Install-Module -Name ModuleName -RequiredVersion 2.0.0

The -Scope parameter specifies the installation scope. For instance, if you're not running PowerShell as an administrator or want the module just for yourself, you'd opt for the 'CurrentUser' scope.

Install-Module -Name ModuleName -Scope CurrentUser

Sometimes, modules are stored in private repositories. In such cases, you must register these repositories beforehand.

Register-PSRepository -Name 'MyRepo' -SourceLocation 'http://myrepo.local'

After registering, you can specify the repository while installing the module:

Install-Module -Name ModuleName -Repository 'MyRepo'

Manual Installation

While the PowerShell Gallery is convenient, there will be instances where you'll need to install modules manually, perhaps due to security reasons or because the module isn't available on public repositories.

Manually downloaded modules must be placed in a specific directory listed in $env:PSModulePath. It's crucial to maintain a well-organized structure; else, you risk module conflicts or versioning issues.

Once the module files are in place, you need to import them.

Import-Module ModulePath

These manually installed modules may require other modules or libraries. These dependencies are not automatically resolved, putting the onus on you to verify that everything the module needs is in place. Also, these dependencies are usually documented, but not always.

Resolving Dependencies

The -Force flag can be a lifesaver as it automatically resolves dependencies when installing from the PowerShell Gallery.

Install-Module -Name ComplexModule -Force

When installing modules manually, you need to be even more cautious. Each dependency must be downloaded and placed in the appropriate directory, or else you risk a failed installation or reduced functionality.

In enterprise settings, network configurations like firewalls and proxies can hinder module installations. The -Proxy parameter is your friend in such situations:

Install-Module -Name ModuleName -Proxy 'http://proxyserver:8080'

Debugging Installations

When all else fails, debugging is your last resort. Commands like Get-Error can be invaluable, as they provide a detailed report of what went wrong during the installation.

Get-Error

Many PowerShell modules are also packaged using NuGet, a package manager for the Microsoft development platform. You may sometimes need to install or update the NuGet provider for successful module installation.

Install-PackageProvider -Name NuGet -Force

Gaining a thorough understanding of each of these areas will provide you the tools you need to install even the most advanced PowerShell modules. When it comes to versioning, dependencies, environments, permissions, proxies, or debugging, each element comes with its own unique challenges and solutions. With this knowledge, you'll be able to confidently handle even the most complex installation scenarios.

Module Management

Managing modules encompasses various aspects like versioning, dependencies, maintenance, and security.

We shall explore each of these facets in detail.

Module Inventory

Your first step in module management should be inventory. Being unaware of what modules are installed can lead to conflicts and vulnerabilities. You can get a detailed list of all installed modules using the following command:

```
Get-Module -ListAvailable
```

Version Management

PowerShell allows multiple versions of the same module to exist on a system, a boon and a curse. While it offers flexibility, it also opens the door for version conflicts. You need to actively manage these versions to avoid chaos. Use the following command to list all versions of a specific module:

```
Get-Module -ListAvailable -Name 'ModuleName'
```

Module Dependencies

As we learned earlier, complex modules often have dependencies. Failing to manage these dependencies can result in broken functionalities. While -Force can resolve dependencies, you may want to manually manage them in certain cases, especially for security audits or compliance. The Get-Command utility can help to determine what commands a specific module is providing:

```
Get-Command -Module 'ModuleName'
```

Updates

Regular updates are necessary for security patches and new features. However, updating a module is not always straightforward and can affect the entire system. The Update-Module cmdlet is your friend here:

```
Update-Module -Name 'ModuleName'
```

Uninstallation and Cleanup

Over time, your environment will accumulate old or unused modules. Such modules are not just space-consumers; they can be security risks. Regular clean-up is a healthy practice. You can uninstall a module using:

```
Uninstall-Module -Name 'ModuleName'
```

And the most important thing is documentation which is often seen as tedious but is indispensable for proper module management. Keeping a record of why a certain version of a module is necessary for your projects, or why a module was uninstalled. These records can be invaluable for troubleshooting and auditing.

Create Custom Cmdlets

You can design unique functions in PowerShell that are suited to your own requirements by creating custom cmdlets. You can bundle these custom cmdlets into modules to make them more reusable and easier to distribute. We shall now explore the steps involved in creating, using, and launching personalized cmdlets.

Before we dive into coding, it's important to grasp the fundamental structure of a cmdlet. A cmdlet is typically made up of a Verb-Noun pair and is commonly implemented as a .NET class that derives from Cmdlet or PSCmdlet. Actions are represented by verbs, while entities that undergo the actions are represented by nouns.

Development Environment

PowerShell doesn't require a specialized IDE for cmdlet development. However, if you're comfortable with Visual Studio, it does offer robust debugging and IntelliSense features. Regardless of your choice, you'll need the PowerShell SDK. It provides the necessary libraries to compile your code into cmdlets.

Starting with a basic "HelloWorld" cmdlet will be our first task. To begin, create a C# class library project and include a reference to System.Effective management.Automation.dll.

Following is the snippet to define a basic cmdlet:

```csharp
using System.Management.Automation;

[Cmdlet(VerbsCommon.Get, "HelloWorld")]
public class HelloWorldCmdlet : Cmdlet
{
    protected override void ProcessRecord()
    {
        WriteObject("Hello, World!");
    }
}
```

The [Cmdlet] attribute specifies the Verb and Noun. The ProcessRecord method is where the cmdlet's action is performed.

Compiling and Testing

Once your code is ready, compile the project to generate a DLL file. Load this DLL into your PowerShell session using Import-Module:

```
Import-Module ./path/to/your/dll
```

Now, you should be able to run Get-HelloWorld and see "Hello, World!" outputted to the terminal.

Parameters

The cmdlets usually have parameters to make them flexible. You can define parameters in your cmdlet class like this:

```
[Parameter(Position = 0, Mandatory = true)]
public string Name { get; set; }
```

In ProcessRecord, you can now use this Name property:

```
WriteObject($"Hello, {Name}!");
```

Validation and Error Handling

Adding validation attributes can ensure that the inputs are as expected. For example, [ValidateNotNullOrEmpty] ensures that the parameter value is neither null nor an empty string. Moreover, to handle errors gracefully, use ThrowTerminatingError for terminating errors and WriteError for non-terminating errors.

```
if(string.IsNullOrEmpty(Name))
{
   ThrowTerminatingError(
      new ErrorRecord(
         new ArgumentNullException("Name"),
```

```
            "NameNullOrEmpty",
            ErrorCategory.InvalidArgument,
            null
        )
    );
}
```

Pipelining

PowerShell also allows data to be passed from one cmdlet to another through a pipeline. You can enable this feature in your custom cmdlet by overriding the ProcessRecord method and using the ValueFromPipeline property in the Parameter attribute:

```
[Parameter(ValueFromPipeline = true)]
public object InputObject { get; set; }
```

Your custom cmdlet can also have initialization and cleanup routines using the BeginProcessing and EndProcessing methods:

```
protected override void BeginProcessing()
{
    // Initialization code here
}


protected override void EndProcessing()
{
    // Cleanup code here
}
```

You can customize your PowerShell environment to exactly meet your needs if you know how to construct custom cmdlets. You may encapsulate functionality in a clean, reusable, and distributable form with custom cmdlets, regardless of how basic or complex the workflow is. This capability takes PowerShell beyond being just a scripting language and transforms it into a comprehensive development platform.

Advanced Custom Cmdlet

Let us now look at constructing a more complex custom cmdlet. We will make a cmdlet that can handle all the necessary operations (Create, Read, Update, Delete) on a mock database stored in a dictionary in-memory. We shall call this cmdlet as Invoke-CrudOperation.

For demonstration purposes, we will use a simple C# dictionary to store key-value pairs. You can use the cmdlet to specify the type of operation, along with the key and value.

Following is the C# code to define our complex cmdlet:

```
using System;
using System.Collections.Generic;
using System.Management.Automation;

namespace CustomCmdletDemo
{
    [Cmdlet(VerbsLifecycle.Invoke, "CrudOperation")]
    public class CrudOperationCmdlet : Cmdlet
    {
        [Parameter(Position = 0, Mandatory = true)]
        [ValidateSet("Create", "Read", "Update", "Delete")]
        public string Operation { get; set; }

        [Parameter(Position = 1, Mandatory = true)]
        public string Key { get; set; }

        [Parameter(Position = 2)]
        public string Value { get; set; }
```

```csharp
    private static Dictionary<string, string> mockDatabase = new Dictionary<string, string>();

    protected override void ProcessRecord()
    {
        switch (Operation)
        {
            case "Create":
                if (mockDatabase.ContainsKey(Key))
                {
                    WriteError(new ErrorRecord(
                        new InvalidOperationException($"Key '{Key}' already exists."),
                        "KeyExists",
                        ErrorCategory.ResourceExists,
                        Key));
                    return;
                }
                mockDatabase[Key] = Value;
                WriteObject($"Created: Key = {Key}, Value = {Value}");
                break;

            case "Read":
                if (!mockDatabase.TryGetValue(Key, out string readValue))
                {
                    WriteError(new ErrorRecord(
                        new KeyNotFoundException($"Key '{Key}' not found."),
                        "KeyNotFound",
                        ErrorCategory.ObjectNotFound,
                        Key));
```

```csharp
                return;
            }
            WriteObject($"Read: Key = {Key}, Value = {readValue}");
            break;

        case "Update":
            if (!mockDatabase.ContainsKey(Key))
            {
                WriteError(new ErrorRecord(
                    new KeyNotFoundException($"Key '{Key}' not found."),
                    "KeyNotFound",
                    ErrorCategory.ObjectNotFound,
                    Key));
                return;
            }
            mockDatabase[Key] = Value;
            WriteObject($"Updated: Key = {Key}, Value = {Value}");
            break;

        case "Delete":
            if (!mockDatabase.Remove(Key))
            {
                WriteError(new ErrorRecord(
                    new KeyNotFoundException($"Key '{Key}' not found."),
                    "KeyNotFound",
                    ErrorCategory.ObjectNotFound,
                    Key));
                return;
```

```
                }
                WriteObject($"Deleted: Key = {Key}");
                break;

            default:
                throw new ArgumentException("Invalid operation type");
        }
    }
  }
}
```

In the above script, we have three parameters: Operation, Key, and Value. Operation can be one of the CRUD operations and is mandatory. Key is also mandatory, while Value is optional.

We are using a static Dictionary to simulate a database. This dictionary is shared among all instances of the cmdlet. Inside the ProcessRecord method, we perform the specified CRUD operation based on the Operation parameter. We then use WriteError to write any errors and WriteObject to write the results.

After that, to put into use, we compile this code into a DLL as before. Then, import the module in PowerShell as below:

Import-Module ./path/to/your/dll

Following are some of the examples:

- Create an Entry: Invoke-CrudOperation -Operation Create -Key "Name" -Value "John"

- Read an Entry: Invoke-CrudOperation -Operation Read -Key "Name"

- Update an Entry: Invoke-CrudOperation -Operation Update -Key "Name" -Value "Doe"

- Delete an Entry: Invoke-CrudOperation -Operation Delete -Key "Name"

This sophisticated cmdlet shows you how to manage various operations, parameters, and failures. The design is modular, allowing for easy extension of functionality and adaptation to real-world database operations.

Perform Error Handling

Effective error handling in PowerShell cmdlets is essential for a well-designed cmdlet. It guarantees that users receive helpful information when issues arise. In the previous example, we saw how the Invoke-CrudOperation cmdlet was used to output error messages using WriteError. We will give another look to this WriteError method as below:

Using WriteError Method

This method allows you to specify errors in a detailed manner using an ErrorRecord object. You can specify the error message, the category of the error, and a target object that the error is associated with. In our Invoke-CrudOperation example, WriteError was used as follows:

```
WriteError(new ErrorRecord(
    new InvalidOperationException($"Key '{Key}' already exists."),
    "KeyExists",
    ErrorCategory.ResourceExists,
    Key));
```

In the above, InvalidOperationException is the exception object, "KeyExists" is the error ID, ErrorCategory.ResourceExists is the category, and Key is the target object.

Implementing Try-Catch Blocks

You can implement a try-catch block to handle terminating type of errors which stops the cmdlet's execution and return control to the user.. Within the catch block, you can use WriteError to write an ErrorRecord.

For example, we shall modify the "Update" case in our previous Invoke-CrudOperation cmdlet to add a try-catch block:

```
case "Update":
    try
    {
        if (!mockDatabase.ContainsKey(Key))
```

```
        {
            throw new KeyNotFoundException($"Key '{Key}' not found.");
        }
        mockDatabase[Key] = Value;
        WriteObject($"Updated: Key = {Key}, Value = {Value}");
    }
    catch (Exception e)
    {
        WriteError(new ErrorRecord(
            e,
            "UpdateFailed",
            ErrorCategory.WriteError,
            Key));
    }
    break;
```

In the above code snippet, we used try-catch to handle errors during the "Update" operation. If the key is not found in the database, a KeyNotFoundException is thrown, caught in the catch block, and an error record is written.

It's important to remember that errors written with WriteError can be captured downstream in the error pipeline by the user for further actions.

Summary

We explored various aspects of PowerShell modules and cmdlets in this chapter. We began by examining modules and their three types: script, binary, and manifest modules. Each type has a distinct role in packaging, distributing, and utilizing PowerShell functionalities. We also explored the installation of modules, particularly those that can be tricky, like modules with dependencies or ones that require specific permissions. We also placed a strong emphasis on management practices related to modules. This included ensuring concise and organized version control, regular updates, and implementing best practices to avoid any conflicts that may arise with the modules.

Moving on to cmdlets, the chapter offered valuable information on how to create your own custom cmdlets. We explored the relationship between cmdlets and the PowerShell runtime, highlighting their close connection as specialized .NET classes. The chapter provided an example using the Invoke-CrudOperation cmdlet to demonstrate how to simplify complex logic while ensuring user-friendly functionality. This was also expanded to showcase another intricate cmdlet, highlighting its relevance in practical scenarios.

There was also significant focus on error handling in cmdlets. We covered the two types of errors: terminating and non-terminating, as well as ways to effectively deal with them. The importance of using WriteError, throw, and try-catch mechanisms was emphasized, as well as the significance of providing meaningful error messages and categories. We also learned the $ErrorActionPreference automatic variable in PowerShell and how it applies to custom cmdlets. Real-life examples were used to showcase how these concepts can be applied, such as making changes to the Invoke-CrudOperation cmdlet.

Chapter 5: Scripting in PowerShell

PowerShell Scripting Overview

To ensure that you leave this chapter with a solid grasp of PowerShell scripting, we will go over a wide variety of subjects. We shall begin by understanding the fundamentals of PowerShell scripting and how it differs from basic command-line executions. This will provide a foundation for delving further into the details of scripting, such as variables and data types, which are essential components. You'll discover how to work with a variety of data types, including arrays, strings, and integers, as well as how to employ different kinds of variables.

We will then concentrate on conditional statements, which manage a script's flow of execution. By utilizing if, else, and switch statements, you can establish conditions for various scenarios. Next, loops and iteration, with particular attention paid to constructs like for, foreach, while, and do-while that enable scripts to efficiently carry out repetitive operations. You will learn how to make your scripts more flexible and dynamic by managing the way loops and exit conditions flow.

The chapter will also cover the concept of functions and parameters. We will explore the process of breaking down your code into smaller, more manageable parts by organizing it into functions. Additionally, we will learn ways to enhance the versatility and ease of use of these functions by incorporating parameters. You will discover how to define functions, call them, pass parameters to them, and get their return values.

In keeping with recommended practices, the chapter will teach error management in scripts. We will go over how to use try, catch, finally, and throw blocks to identify, trap, and manage failures. We will also look at PowerShell's error variables and cmdlets for efficient debugging.

Finally, we will conclude the chapter by providing a brief summary of script execution policies in PowerShell. You'll learn about the various script security tiers, including Unrestricted, AllSigned, RemoteSigned, and Restricted, as well as how to adjust or change these standards.

Advantages of PowerShell Scripting

PowerShell scripting and command-line executions serve different purposes and offer distinct advantages. While both environments allow you to interact with the system and execute tasks, they do so in fundamentally different ways, offering unique advantages and limitations.

Flexibility
In PowerShell scripting, you can automate complex tasks and procedures by writing comprehensive scripts. This flexibility allows you to perform operations like reading and writing files, making API calls, or even deploying entire server configurations, which goes well beyond simple command-line instructions.

Modularity
Scripting supports the creation of reusable code blocks and functions. You can create a function to accomplish a specific task and then call that function multiple times within the script or in other scripts. This modular approach aids in maintaining and troubleshooting code by centralizing the logic.

Scheduled Execution
Scripts can be set to run at scheduled times using services like Task Scheduler. This is useful for maintenance tasks that need to occur during off-hours, such as backups, updates, or system scans.

Conditional Logic
Scripts support conditional statements (if, else, switch), loops (for, foreach, while, do-while), and exception handling (try, catch, finally). These elements allow for more complex and flexible program flows compared to a straightforward command-line execution.

User Interactivity
You can design your script to be interactive, prompting the user for input or decisions during execution. This allows the script to adapt to various conditions or requirements, making it more versatile.

The degree of complexity they are intended to manage is where they diverge most. When doing a single, isolated job that doesn't need conditional logic or repeated execution, command-line executions are frequently utilized. On the other hand, PowerShell scripting provides a robust feature set that facilitates modularity, rational decision-making, and the automation of difficult tasks. For example, to verify connectivity when troubleshooting a network problem, you can use the ping command. However, PowerShell scripting would be more suited if you wanted to develop a report that applies conditional logic, gets data from several services, and publishes the outcome to a file.

PowerShell Variables

Variables are an integral part of PowerShell scripting, acting as placeholders to store data that can be used and manipulated throughout the script. In PowerShell, a variable is declared using the $ symbol followed by the variable name. The name can consist of letters, numbers, and underscores but must not start with a number.

$myVariable = "Hello, world!"

$number1 = 10

$booleanValue = $true

Data Types

Although PowerShell is dynamically typed, meaning it automatically determines the data type of a variable, you can explicitly define the type if needed.

[string]$name = "John"

[int]$age = 30

[boolean]$isOnline = $false

String Manipulation

Strings in PowerShell can be manipulated in various ways. For instance, you can concatenate strings using the + operator or format them using the -f operator. Assume or consider that we want to dynamically build a URL:

$baseUrl = "http://www.example.com"

$resource = "/api/resource"

$fullUrl = $baseUrl + $resource

Array and Hash Tables

Arrays and hash tables allow you to store multiple values in a single variable.

```
# Array
$colors = @("Red", "Green", "Blue")

# Hash Table
$user = @{
  Name = "John"
  Age = 30
}
```

Accessing Variables

You can access array elements or hash table values using indexes and keys, respectively.

```
# Array
$firstColor = $colors[0]


# Hash Table
$userName = $user["Name"]
```

Using Variables in Scripts

Variables can be used to store user input, intermediate results, or configuration data. Consider a script to perform basic math operations:

```
$number1 = Read-Host "Enter the first number"
$number2 = Read-Host "Enter the second number"

$sum = $number1 + $number2
$product = $number1 * $number2

Write-Host "Sum: $sum"
Write-Host "Product: $product"
```

PowerShell also allows access to system environment variables using the Env: drive.

```
$path = $Env:PATH
```

Scope of Variables

Variables can have different scopes such as global, script, or local, defining where they can be accessed or modified. For instance, a global variable can be accessed from any part of the script or even from the PowerShell session.

```
$global:myGlobalVariable = "I am global"
$script:myScriptVariable = "I am script-wide"
$local:myLocalVariable = "I am local to this function or script block"
```

Special Variables

PowerShell has several built-in variables like $_, $PSVersionTable, or $PWD that hold specific types of data. For example, $_ is used in loops and pipelines to refer to the current object, and $PSVersionTable stores details about the PowerShell environment.

Get-Process | ForEach-Object { Write-Host $_.Name }

Data Types in Practice

In any programming or scripting language, including PowerShell, data types are essential. Working with various data types enables you to manage and manipulate data effectively, strengthening and adapting your scripts.

Using Basic Data Types

Following are some of the fundamental data types you definitely want to be known to be working with:

- Integers (int): Used for whole numbers.

[int]$wholeNumber = 42

- Floating-Point Numbers (double): For numbers with decimal points.

[double]$floatingNumber = 42.42

- Boolean (bool): Stores True or False.

[bool]$flag = $true

- Strings (string): Used for textual data.

[string]$text = "PowerShell"

Using Collections

PowerShell also offers collection data types, such as arrays and hash tables, which can store multiple values.

- Arrays: Ordered collection of items, which can be of mixed types.

$myArray = @(1, 2, 3, "text")

- Hash Tables: Key-value pairs used for structured data storage.

$myHashTable = @{ "Key1" = "Value1"; "Key2" = 42 }

Using Type Conversion and Casting

In various situations and enterprise needs, you'll need to convert from one data type to another. PowerShell allows both implicit and explicit type conversions. For example, when you perform operations between different numeric types, PowerShell implicitly converts them.

$intVar = 3
$doubleVar = 1.2
$result = $intVar * $doubleVar # Implicitly converts $intVar to double

Explicit conversion can be done using casting:

[string]$intValue = 42 # converts integer to string

Using Type Constraints and Validation

You can impose type constraints on variables to ensure that only certain types of data get stored. Type constraints can also be used with function parameters to ensure that the incoming data matches what the function expects.

function Display-Age ([int]$age) {
    Write-Host "Your age is $age."
}

Calling Display-Age with a non-integer value will throw a type mismatch error, thus making your code safer.

Using Nullable Types

In some cases, you may want to allow a variable to hold a null value along with its regular data type. PowerShell supports nullable types for this purpose.

[nullable[int]]$nullableInt = $null

Dynamic Type Checking

PowerShell allows for dynamic type checking, where the type of a variable is determined at runtime. While this offers flexibility, it can sometimes lead to unexpected errors if not handled carefully.

$dynamicVar = "string"

$dynamicVar = $dynamicVar * 2   # Error as PowerShell interprets $dynamicVar as a string

Type Literals

PowerShell allows you to make use of type literals to perform operations or create instances without explicitly storing the type in a variable.

[System.Math]::Sqrt(25)   # Calls the Sqrt static method on the System.Math class

The GetType() Method

You can use the GetType() method to find out the type of a variable at runtime, which is particularly useful in debugging scenarios.

$var = 42

$var.GetType().Name   # Output: Int32

Enumerations

PowerShell allows for the definition and usage of enumerations, which are a way to assign names to numeric values, making your code more readable and self-explanatory.

```
enum Colors {
    Red = 1
    Green = 2
    Blue = 3
}
```

Here-Strings

When working with large blocks of text, the Here-String data type can be convenient. It allows for the inclusion of multiple lines and special characters without the need for escape sequences.

```
$hereString = @"
This is a multiple
line string.
"@
```

Custom Classes

Advanced users may also define custom classes in PowerShell scripts. These custom classes can contain properties and methods.

```
class Person {
    [string]$Name
    [int]$Age
    [void]SayHello() {
        Write-Host "Hello, my name is $($this.Name)"
    }
}
```

Tuples and Custom Value Types

Tuples are a quick way to group multiple values of possibly different types. They are not native

PowerShell types but can be created using .NET classes.

$tuple = [Tuple]::Create('John', 32)

Record Types

PowerShell doesn't directly support record types, but you can mimic them using custom objects or hash tables to hold a fixed set of related items.

```
$record = [PSCustomObject]@{
    ID = 1
    Name = "John"
}
```

PowerShell scripting requires a thorough understanding of data types. Knowing how to use each of the basic integer and string types, as well as more complex collections and custom classes, can significantly improve the capabilities of your scripting technique in your system administration tasks.

Introduction to Conditional Statements

Conditional statements are the cornerstone of any scripting or programming language, allowing you to introduce decision-making capabilities into your scripts. In PowerShell, the primary constructs for condition-based logic are if, elseif, else, switch, and ternary operators.

if, elseif, and else Statements

The if statement is the most straightforward. It executes a block of code if the condition specified returns true.

```
$var = 10
if ($var -eq 10) {
    Write-Host "Variable is 10."
}
```

You can expand upon this with elseif and else to handle more conditions:

```
$var = 20
if ($var -eq 10) {
    Write-Host "Variable is 10."
} elseif ($var -eq 20) {
    Write-Host "Variable is 20."
} else {
    Write-Host "Variable is neither 10 nor 20."
}
```

switch Statement

The switch statement in PowerShell allows you to perform multiple checks using a cleaner and more organized syntax.

```
var = "Apple"
switch ($var) {
    "Apple" {
        Write-Host "It's an apple."
    }
    "Banana" {
        Write-Host "It's a banana."
    }
    default {
        Write-Host "It's neither an apple nor a banana."
    }
}
```

Wildcards and Regular Expressions

One unique feature of PowerShell's switch statement is the ability to use wildcards and regular expressions for pattern matching:

```
$var = "Bread"
switch -Wildcard ($var) {
  "Br*" {
    Write-Host "Starts with Br."
  }
}
```

Ternary Operator

A lesser-known conditional operator in PowerShell is the ternary operator, which allows for shorter conditional expressions:

```
$var = 10
$result = ($var -eq 10) ? "Ten" : "Not Ten"
```

Nested Conditions

Conditions can also be nested within each other for complex logic. However, too much nesting can make the code hard to read and maintain.

```
$var1 = 10
$var2 = 20
if ($var1 -eq 10) {
  if ($var2 -eq 20) {
    Write-Host "Both variables are correct."
  }
}
```

Where-Object Cmdlet

While not a traditional conditional statement, Where-Object acts as a filter, allowing you to pass through only objects that satisfy a certain condition. It's most commonly used in pipelines.

```
$numbers = 1..10
```

$evenNumbers = $numbers | Where-Object { $_ % 2 -eq 0 }

Conditional Execution with && and ||
PowerShell 7 introduced the && and || operators, allowing you to chain commands based on the success or failure of a preceding command.

Get-Process 'chrome' && Write-Host 'Chrome is running.'

Exit Codes and $?
Every PowerShell command returns an exit code ($?), which can be utilized to make decisions.

Get-Process 'notepad'
if ($? -eq $true) {
    Write-Host 'Notepad is running.'
}

Sample Program: Using Conditional Statement
Once we have a firm grasp on the fundamentals, we can delve further into the real-world uses of conditional statements in PowerShell scripts, highlighting specific examples of when these constructs prove to be invaluable. We will expand on an IT automation example, which is essentially a PowerShell script that checks if certain software and services are running on a server.

Multi-Condition Checks
Imagine you're tasked with monitoring a server that should be running specific services like HTTP and SQL Server. You could use nested if statements to create multi-conditions.

$services = Get-Service | Select-Object -Property 'Status','ServiceName'
if ($services | Where-Object {$_.ServiceName -eq 'w3svc' -and $_.Status -eq 'Running'})
{
   if ($services | Where-Object {$_.ServiceName -eq 'MSSQLSERVER' -and $_.Status -eq 'Running'}) {
       Write-Host "Both HTTP and SQL Server services are running."

        }
}
```

This nested condition ensures both HTTP and SQL Server services are active.

## *Leveraging switch for Log Monitoring*

Imagine that you have a log file where different types of events are registered as "INFO," "WARN," or "ERROR." You want to apply different actions based on these event types.

```
$logEntries = Get-Content C:\Path\To\Log\File.log
foreach ($entry in $logEntries) {
    switch -Regex ($entry) {
        "INFO" {
            # Code to handle INFO
        }
        "WARN" {
            # Code to send warning email
        }
        "ERROR" {
            # Code to send error email and restart service
        }
    }
}
```

The switch statement with regular expressions can scan through log entries and apply specific actions based on the type of log event.

Ternary Operators for Quick Decisions

Consider that you have a script that either performs a backup or deletes old backup files based on available disk space.

```
$diskSpace = Get-FreeDiskSpace # Assume this function returns free disk space in GB
```
```

$action = ($diskSpace -lt 100) ? "DELETE" : "BACKUP"

This quick decision-making is possible because of the terseness of the ternary operator.

The Utility of $?
Suppose you execute a Copy-Item command in your script to duplicate a database backup file. You want to check if it was successful.

Copy-Item C:\Path\To\DBBackup.sql C:\Path\To\NewFolder\
if ($? -eq $true) {
    # Further actions like sending a confirmation email
}

Combining Where-Object with if
You can filter services that are running and then use if to check if that list includes a specific service, like IIS.

runningServices = Get-Service | Where-Object { $_.Status -eq 'Running' }
if ($runningServices.ServiceName -contains 'w3svc') {
    # Actions if IIS is running
}

Exploiting Exit Codes with && and ||
In PowerShell 7, you can use these to execute commands conditionally based on the success of previous ones.

Test-Connection google.com -Count 1 && Invoke-WebRequest http://google.com || Write-Host "No internet."

This command will ping Google; if successful, it will send an HTTP request. If the ping fails, it'll print "No internet."

These examples demonstrate the practical uses of conditional statements in PowerShell, showcasing how you can adapt these constructs to various real-world scenarios similar to what have been demonstrated in this practical example.

Understanding Loops and Iteration

Loops are essential for performing repetitive tasks until a particular condition is met or for iterating through collections like arrays or hashes. We will continue using the IT automation example of checking services on a server, which was introduced in the previous section about conditional statements to further understand the role of loops and iterations..

Using for Loops for Scheduled Maintenance Checks

In an enterprise environment, you might need to perform checks on multiple servers at fixed intervals. The for loop is ideal for such tasks:

```
$servers = @("Server1", "Server2", "Server3")
for ($i = 0; $i -lt $servers.length; $i++) {
    $server = $servers[$i]
    Write-Host "Checking services on $server..."
    # Service check code here
}
```

Here, the for loop runs through the list of servers, invoking the service check code for each.

Utilizing foreach Loop for Array Iteration

If you have a list of services that you need to ensure are running on each server, you can use a foreach loop. This loop is easier to read and write when you're working with collections:

```
$servicesToCheck = @('w3svc', 'MSSQLSERVER', 'SMTPSVC')
foreach ($service in $servicesToCheck) {
    Write-Host "Checking $service..."
    # Service check code here
}
```

This loop iterates through each service in the list, enabling you to invoke specific checks or actions for each one.

Implementing while Loop for Conditional Repetition

The while loop is generally used for situations where you need to perform a task until a particular condition is met. Imagine a scenario where you need to keep checking whether a new log entry has been added to a server log:

```
while ((Get-Content -Path "C:\Path\To\Log\File.log").Count -le 100) {
    Start-Sleep -Seconds 5
    Write-Host "Waiting for new log entries..."
}
```

This loop will keep running as long as the log file has 100 or fewer lines, sleeping for 5 seconds between each iteration.

Employing do-while and do-until for Postcondition Loops

Sometimes you might need to execute the loop at least once before checking a condition. This is where do-while and do-until loops come into play.

```
do {
    $lineCount = (Get-Content -Path "C:\Path\To\Log\File.log").Count
    Write-Host "Current line count: $lineCount"
    Start-Sleep -Seconds 5
}
while ($lineCount -le 100)
```

Here, the loop will execute at least once, updating the line count and then checking the condition.

Pipeline Iteration with ForEach-Object

PowerShell's pipeline can be harnessed to perform actions on each object flowing through it:

```
Get-Process | ForEach-Object {
    if ($_.WorkingSet64 -gt 100MB) {
        Write-Host "Process $_.Name is consuming more than 100MB of memory."
    }
}
```

}

In the above snippet, the ForEach-Object cmdlet is used to iterate over each process object passed down the pipeline. It checks if any process is consuming more than 100MB of memory and notifies you if it finds any.

Breaking and Continuing Loops

PowerShell provides two key words, break and continue, to control loop execution dynamically. break exits the loop entirely, whereas continue skips the current iteration and moves to the next:

```
for ($i = 1; $i -le 10; $i++) {
    if ($i % 2 -eq 0) {
        continue
    }
    Write-Host "Processing odd number: $i"
}
```

In the above snippet, the loop will skip even numbers, and the output will only show odd numbers between 1 and 10. Through examples like server checks and log monitoring, it becomes clear that these constructs have practical applications that can significantly streamline routine IT tasks.

Diving into Functions and Parameters

PowerShell functions are similar to mini-scripts in that they can be reused and accept parameters. In this section, we will look at how to write basic, parameterized, and advanced functions that use parameters with various attributes.

Simplifying Code Blocks

The first step in understanding functions is looking at their most basic form. Imagine a block of code that checks if a particular service is running on a local machine:

```
$serviceName = 'w3svc'
$serviceStatus = Get-Service -Name $serviceName | Select-Object -ExpandProperty Status
Write-Host "Status of $serviceName is $serviceStatus"
```

Rather than writing these lines repeatedly, you can encapsulate them in a function:

```
function Check-ServiceStatus {
    $serviceName = 'w3svc'
    $serviceStatus = Get-Service -Name $serviceName | Select-Object -ExpandProperty Status
    Write-Host "Status of $serviceName is $serviceStatus"
}
```

To invoke this function, you simply call its name:

Check-ServiceStatus

Parameterized Functions: Adding Flexibility

While the above example simplifies code repetition, it lacks flexibility. Parameterized functions accept one or more parameters, making them far more versatile:

```
function Check-ServiceStatus {
    param (
        [string]$serviceName
    )
    $serviceStatus = Get-Service -Name $serviceName | Select-Object -ExpandProperty Status
    Write-Host "Status of $serviceName is $serviceStatus"
}
```

To call this function, you pass the service name as an argument:

```
Check-ServiceStatus -serviceName 'w3svc'
```

Cmdlet Binding and Parameters

You will often come across advanced functions that leverage the CmdletBinding attribute and use various parameter attributes:

```
function Get-DiskSpaceInfo {
    [CmdletBinding()]
    param (
        [Parameter(Mandatory=$true)]
        [string]$driveLetter,

        [Parameter(Mandatory=$false)]
        [switch]$detailed
    )

    $diskInfo = Get-Volume -DriveLetter $driveLetter
```

```
    if ($detailed) {
        $diskInfo | Select-Object *
    } else {
        $diskInfo | Select-Object DriveLetter, FileSystem, Size, SizeRemaining
    }
}
```

In this function, $driveLetter is a mandatory parameter, while $detailed is optional. The function returns disk space information based on these parameters:

Get-DiskSpaceInfo -driveLetter 'C' -detailed

Using Parameter Sets for Overloaded Functions

Sometimes you might want a function to perform different actions based on the parameters provided. PowerShell allows for this through parameter sets:

```
function Get-ServerInfo {
    [CmdletBinding(DefaultParameterSetName='ByName')]
    param (
        [Parameter(Mandatory=$true, ParameterSetName='ByName')]
        [string]$serverName,

        [Parameter(Mandatory=$true, ParameterSetName='ByIP')]
        [string]$ipAddress
    )

    if ($PSCmdlet.ParameterSetName -eq 'ByName') {
        # Code to get server info by name
    } else {
        # Code to get server info by IP
```

        }
}

This function can be invoked either by serverName or ipAddress, but not both. This is controlled by the ParameterSetName attribute.

Pipeline Support in Functions

Last but not least, functions in PowerShell can accept input from the pipeline. To do this, you must define a process block inside the function:

```
function Stop-TargetService {
    [CmdletBinding()]
    param (
        [Parameter(Mandatory=$true, ValueFromPipeline=$true)]
        [string]$serviceName
    )

    process {
        Stop-Service -Name $serviceName
    }
}
```

Now you can pipe service names into this function:

```
@('w3svc', 'MSSQLSERVER') | Stop-TargetService
```

These functions facilitate code reuse, allow for flexible input through parameters, and can even work in tandem with other PowerShell cmdlets through pipeline integration.

Dealing with Errors

When writing PowerShell scripts, dealing with errors is unavoidable. You're dealing with systems that may have varying configurations, intermittent network connectivity, and external dependencies. To write robust and resilient scripts, you must understand PowerShell's error-handling mechanisms. We will explore the most basic forms of error handling, including $ErrorActionPreference, Try-Catch-Finally blocks, and terminating and non-terminating errors.

Terminating vs. Non-terminating Errors

PowerShell has two types of errors—terminating and non-terminating. Terminating errors halt script execution, while non-terminating errors allow the script to continue. Understanding this distinction is crucial when automating tasks.

For example, we shall consider a function that retrieves service status:

```
function Get-ServiceStatus {
  param (
    [string]$serviceName
  )
  Get-Service -Name $serviceName | Select-Object -ExpandProperty Status
}
```

If the service does not exist, Get-Service will throw a non-terminating error, and the script will proceed, which might not be desirable.

Try-Catch-Finally

The Try-Catch-Finally block provides a structured way to capture and deal with errors. Inside the Try block, you put the code that might cause an error. The Catch block catches the error and defines what actions to take. The Finally block contains code that will always execute, regardless of an error.

We shall modify the above Get-ServiceStatus function:

```
function Get-ServiceStatus {
  param (
    [string]$serviceName
  )
  try {
```

```
    $status = Get-Service -Name $serviceName -ErrorAction Stop | Select-Object -ExpandProperty Status
    Write-Host "Status of $serviceName is $status."
  } catch {
    Write-Host "An error occurred: $_"
  } finally {
    Write-Host "Done checking service."
  }
}
```

By setting -ErrorAction Stop, we promote the non-terminating error to a terminating one, allowing it to be caught in the Catch block.

$ErrorActionPreference

Setting $ErrorActionPreference allows you to define how PowerShell globally handles errors. It has several options like Continue, Stop, SilentlyContinue, and Inquire. Be cautious when using this variable as it can override individual cmdlet behaviors.

For instance, you can set this variable at the beginning of your script:

$ErrorActionPreference = 'Stop'

However, remember that this will affect all cmdlets in the script that do not have an explicit -ErrorAction defined. You can reset it back to its default value (Continue) when you're done with the critical section of your code.

Custom Error Objects

You can also define your custom error messages using Throw and Write-Error. The Throw keyword stops execution and returns a custom error message:

```
if ($diskSpace -lt 500MB) {
    throw "Disk space critically low."
}
```

Write-Error, on the other hand, creates a non-terminating error:

```
if ($cpuUsage -gt 90%) {
    Write-Error "CPU usage critically high."
}
```

As your scripts get more complex and start interacting with different services, databases, or APIs, proper error handling becomes even more critical.

Script Execution Policies

One way PowerShell's script execution policies keep unauthorized users out of a system is by dictating how much trust is necessary to run scripts. These policies protect against executing malicious or unintended code. We will go over the various types of execution policies and show practical examples of how to set and use them.

Types of Execution Policies

There are four main execution policies in PowerShell:

1. Restricted: This is the default policy and doesn't permit any scripts to run, making it the safest option.

2. AllSigned: Requires that all scripts and configuration files be signed by a trusted publisher.

3. RemoteSigned: Allows locally-created scripts to run. Scripts downloaded from the internet or received via email must be signed by a trusted publisher.

4. Unrestricted: Lifts all restrictions and allows any script to run, posing a security risk.

Setting Execution Policies

You can set the execution policy at different scopes—Process, CurrentUser, LocalMachine, or even Undefined to remove any explicitly set policy at a certain scope. The Set-ExecutionPolicy cmdlet is used for this.

For example, if you want to set the execution policy to RemoteSigned for the LocalMachine scope, you'd run:

Set-ExecutionPolicy -ExecutionPolicy RemoteSigned -Scope LocalMachine

Viewing Execution Policies
To see the existing execution policy, you can use the Get-ExecutionPolicy cmdlet:

Get-ExecutionPolicy -List

Let us consider you have a system monitoring script called Monitor-System.ps1 that gathers data about CPU usage, disk space, and running services. Before running the script, you'd like to ensure your execution policy settings are aligned with your security requirements.

Restricted Environment
If you're in a secure environment where policies are stringent, you might need to get the Monitor-System.ps1 script signed by a trusted publisher to run it under the AllSigned policy. Signing the script involves using a certificate and the Set-AuthenticodeSignature cmdlet.

Moderate Restrictions
In a moderately secure environment, you can use the RemoteSigned policy. If your script is downloaded from the internet, unblock it first using the Unblock-File cmdlet before running it.

Unblock-File -Path .\Monitor-System.ps1

Lenient Policy
If the machine on which you're running the script is isolated or you're performing tests, you might set the execution policy to Unrestricted temporarily. However, be aware of the risks involved.

Script-Specific Policy
You could temporarily alter the execution policy just for running the script using the -ExecutionPolicy flag:

powershell.exe -ExecutionPolicy Bypass -File .\Monitor-System.ps1

The precedence order for execution policies is as follows: Process > CurrentUser > LocalMachine. A policy set at a higher-precedence scope will override the policies at lower-precedence scopes.

Summary

The chapter began by explaining the benefits of scripting in PowerShell and how it differs from regular command-line execution. This provided a solid foundation for understanding scripting's power and flexibility in task automation. We investigated the use of variables in PowerShell, including their declaration and utility. The chapter also covered various data types in PowerShell, demonstrating how to use them effectively in scripts.

The chapter delves into various conditional statements such as if, else, and switch, and provides practical examples of how to use them to control script flow. We learned about the importance of loops in scripting, including different types such as while, do-while, and for. Practical examples demonstrated how these loops could be used for repetitive tasks, increasing script efficiency. The chapter covered the creation and use of functions in PowerShell, including how parameters can be passed and managed. This segment emphasized modular scripting, which improves script readability and reusability.

Dealing with unexpected situations is an important aspect of scriptwriting. The chapter taught various error handling strategies in PowerShell scripts to ensure that they are robust and reliable. Understanding and implementing appropriate PowerShell execution policies was learned to ensure scripts run in a secure and controlled environment. The chapter concluded by emphasizing best practices in PowerShell scripting, such as clear code documentation, troubleshooting with verbose and debug features, and adhering to scripting standards for maintainability and efficiency.

Chapter 6: Understanding Automatic Variables

Overview

This chapter directs you through the PowerShell world of automatic variables. These are PowerShell-provided variables that can be used to store specific types of information during script execution or session interactions. Automatic variables provide significant functionality, including error handling and system information retrieval, and do not require explicit declaration or initialization.

Our primary focus will be on some of the most commonly used automatic variables. These include $error, which captures the most recent error details; $host, which provides information about the host program; $profile, which is associated with the current user's profile script; and $null, which represents the absence of a value or a null value. We will also look at $psversiontable, which displays information about the installed PowerShell version; $lastexitcode, which contains the exit code of the last run application; $args, an array of undeclared parameters passed to a script or function; and finally, $myinvocation, which provides information about the current command, such as the script name, line number, and so on.

To make these concepts more tangible, we will use the previous chapter's system-monitoring script as a running example. This script will serve as a foundation for understanding how each of these automatic variables can be applied practically to improve the script's functionality, robustness, and adaptability. This chapter will go into greater detail about each of these automatic variables, covering their functions, possible applications, and how to optimize our running example script by making use of them.

$Error Variable

Robustness and fault tolerance are crucial, and one tool for achieving these goals is the $Error variable. This automatic variable can detect and save errors that occur during script execution. Using the $Error variable in our system-monitoring script can help with debugging and offering insights into what went wrong, when, and how.

The $Error variable contains an array of error objects. The most recent error is at index 0 ($Error[0]), and previous errors follow in the sequence. These error objects are not simply plain text messages; they are rich objects with characteristics such as the line number where the issue occurred, the command that caused the error, and more.

Consider a section of our system-monitoring script where we retrieve the CPU utilization information. For this purpose, we can use the cmdlet Get-WmiObject. In an ideal scenario, the line of code would look like this:

```
$cpuUtilization = (Get-WmiObject win32_processor).LoadPercentage
```

But what if the WMI service is not running or you don't have the appropriate permissions to query this information? This is where $Error comes in.

Right after this line of code, you can inspect $Error[0] to see if any error has been captured.

```
if ($Error[0]) {
    Write-Host "Failed to get CPU Utilization. Error details: $($Error[0].Exception.Message)"
}
```

The $Error[0].Exception.Message will provide the exact error message. You could also go into more detail by exploring other properties of the $Error[0] object like:

- $Error[0].InvocationInfo.Line: Provides the line where the error occurred.
- $Error[0].CategoryInfo.Category: Categorizes the error.

We shall make this more elaborated within the script.

```
try {
    $cpuUtilization = (Get-WmiObject win32_processor).LoadPercentage
}
catch {
    $Error[0] | ForEach-Object {
        Write-Host "Error: $($_.Exception.Message)"
        Write-Host "Line: $($_.InvocationInfo.Line)"
        Write-Host "Category: $($_.CategoryInfo.Category)"
    }
}
```

In this instance, I used a try-catch block to handle exceptions as they occurred. I then run $Error[0] through ForEach-Object to extract and print all of the error's important characteristics. utilizing a try-catch block is not required for utilizing $Error, but it provides more exact control over error handling in the script.

The advantage of utilizing $Error in our system monitoring script is twofold. For starters, it provides rapid feedback during script execution, which allows for quick troubleshooting. Second, if you execute this script as a scheduled job, you may save the error messages to a log file for further auditing or debugging.

$Host and $Profile Variables

$Host Variable

The $Host variable provides detailed information about the host program in which PowerShell is being run. You can use $Host to fetch information like the name of the host, the version of PowerShell you're using, and even the UI culture settings. The significance of this in our system-monitoring script can be multifaceted.

For instance, if the script requires a particular version of PowerShell to execute some advanced cmdlets, $Host.Version can be used to check the version and possibly halt the script if the requirement is not met. Following is how you can incorporate this:

```
if ($Host.Version.Major -lt 5) {
    Write-Host "This script requires PowerShell version 5 or higher."
    exit
}
```

$Profile Variable

If the user has a PowerShell profile script, the $Profile variable links to its location. A profile script is one that executes when your PowerShell session begins. It allows you to define variables, functions, and aliases, as well as load PowerShell modules.

$Profile can be used in our system-monitoring script to save specific settings such as the place where monitoring logs should be saved and the email address to which alerts should be sent. Assume you want to save some of these settings in your profile script for reusability.

First, you can verify if a profile exists for the current user, or create one if it does not:

```
if (Test-Path $Profile) {
    Write-Host "Profile exists at $Profile"
} else {
```

```
    New-Item -Type File -Path $Profile -Force
    Write-Host "Created a new profile at $Profile"
}
```

In your profile, you could then set variables:

```
# Inside your $Profile script
$global:MonitoringLogLocation = "C:\Logs\Monitoring"
$global:AlertEmail = "admin@example.com"
```

Now, back in the system-monitoring script, you can utilize these variables.

```
$logLocation = $global:MonitoringLogLocation
$alertEmail = $global:AlertEmail
```

This provides for greater customization and versatility. A third party utilizing your system-monitoring script in a different environment can modify the necessary configurations in their profile without delving into the script's source code.

By combining these automated variables, you not only make your script more resilient, but also more adaptive to changing user requirements and system circumstances.

$Null Variable

The $Null variable in PowerShell represents a null or empty value. This can be useful in various scenarios, from initial variable assignment to result validation and conditional checks. The $Null variable plays an essential role in situations where the absence of a value is meaningful. In scripting, especially in system monitoring tasks, this can be crucial for accurately interpreting the state of a system or application. For instance, you might be querying a service status or reading from a log file, and a null value could imply that the service isn't running or the log is empty.

Clearing Variables

In a long-running script like a system-monitoring tool, you may want to clear variables periodically to release memory or to reset their state. Setting a variable to $Null effectively removes its content.

```
# Clearing the variable
$cpuUsage = $Null
```

Validating Outputs

Assume your monitoring script does an operation that, if unsuccessful, will produce an error or a null value. You can use $Null to validate the results.

```
# Example: Querying a service
$serviceStatus = Get-Service -Name "WinRM"


# Validate the output
if ($serviceStatus -eq $Null) {
    Write-Host "Failed to retrieve the service status."
    # Log or perform some other operation
}
```

Object Property Checks

Sometimes, you may need to check specific properties of an object returned by a cmdlet. A null property could provide insights into system health or configuration.

```
# Get information about a disk
$diskInfo = Get-Disk | Where-Object { $_.Number -eq 0 }


# Check if FreeSpace property is null
if ($diskInfo.FreeSpace -eq $Null) {
    Write-Host "Could not retrieve free disk space. Check disk."
    # Log or send an alert
}
```

Array and Collection Operations

If you attempt to access an array index that doesn't exist, it returns $Null. This behavior can be used in system monitoring for validation.

$processes = Get-Process

$targetProcess = $processes[1000]

if ($targetProcess -eq $Null) {
    Write-Host "The specified process index is out of range."
    # Take corrective measures
}

Filtering Out $Null Values

You might collect data over time, and some of these might be $Null. If you're performing aggregate functions like sum or average, $Null values could disrupt the calculations.

Assume $latency holds network latency data

$latency = @(10, 20, $Null, 30, $Null)

Filtering out $Null values

$filteredLatency = $latency | Where-Object { $_ -ne $Null }

Now you can perform calculations

$averageLatency = ($filteredLatency -join '+') / $filteredLatency.Count

$Null can be a very efficient way to handle missing or ambiguous data. Imagine you are checking the availability of multiple services in an array. Some might not respond, returning $Null values. You can easily filter these out before deciding to restart services or send an alert.

$PSVersionTable Variable

$PSVersionTable is another significant PowerShell automatic variable. $PSVersionTable contains information about the PowerShell version currently operating, such as the major and minor versions, build version, and other details. The $PSVersionTable variable is quite useful for determining which features are available for use in your script, allowing you to programmatically adapt to the environment.

Information in $PSVersionTable

When you query $PSVersionTable, it returns an object containing multiple properties:

- PSVersion: The full version of PowerShell.

- PSEdition: The edition of PowerShell. This can be 'Desktop' for Windows PowerShell or 'Core' for PowerShell Core.

- BuildVersion: The build version of PowerShell.

- CLRVersion: The version of the Common Language Runtime (CLR) that PowerShell uses, applicable to Windows PowerShell.

- OS: Information about the operating system.

Assume that our system monitoring script makes use of cmdlets or capabilities that are only accessible in specific PowerShell versions. You can do a version check before running certain sections of the script.

```
# Check for minimum PowerShell version
if ($PSVersionTable.PSVersion.Major -lt 5) {
    Write-Host "Skipping certain checks as PowerShell version is less than 5."
}
else {
    # Perform checks that require PSVersion 5 or above
}
```

Conditional Features

You may want to collect specific performance counters or data, but these may only be available in certain PowerShell versions. You can utilize $PSVersionTable to dynamically alter your script's behavior.

```powershell
# Depending on PSVersion, choose a different set of performance counters
$performanceCounters = if ($PSVersionTable.PSVersion.Major -ge 7) {
    "New-CounterSet1", "New-CounterSet2"
} else {
    "Old-CounterSet1", "Old-CounterSet2"
}

# Capture metrics
Get-Counter -Counter $performanceCounters
```

Debugging and Logging

If your monitoring script includes a central logging mechanism, $PSVersionTable can give additional meta-information while logging, which might be useful for future debugging or analysis. Knowing the PowerShell version might help you isolate issues relating to compatibility or feature availability.

```powershell
# Log PSVersion along with other system metrics
$logEntry = @{
    "Timestamp" = Get-Date
    "PSVersion" = $PSVersionTable.PSVersion
    "CPUUsage" = $cpuUsage
    # other metrics
}

# Convert to JSON and write to log
$logEntry | ConvertTo-Json | Out-File -Append -Path "C:\Path\To\Log\File.log"
```

Identifying the Operating Environment

The $PSVersionTable also has information about the OS, which is crucial in system monitoring for tailoring specific OS-level queries or actions.

```
# Use OS information for specific system queries
if ($PSVersionTable.OS -match 'Windows') {
    # Perform Windows-specific operations
} elseif ($PSVersionTable.OS -match 'Linux') {
    # Perform Linux-specific operations
}
```

To summarize, $PSVersionTable provides the context needed for conditional logic, feature selection, and data logging. It helps in fine-tuning the script according to the runtime environment, thereby enhancing its reliability and effectiveness.

$LastExitCode Variable

This is an automatic variable and is primarily used to capture the exit code of the last run native application or external command. Unlike PowerShell cmdlets, which throw exceptions and use $Error for error handling, native applications usually return an exit code that tells the calling program whether the application completed successfully or not. An exit code of 0 typically indicates success, while a non-zero exit code suggests an error.

To execute certain activities in system monitoring, you may need to engage with native tools or external apps, such as checking disk health, performing backups, or running system diagnostics. These tasks do not typically return PowerShell-friendly output or exceptions. Instead, they communicate their success or failure via exit codes, making $LastExitCode an important variable for monitoring script robustness and reliability.

Basic Usage of $LastExitCode

To grasp how $LastExitCode functions, you can use it to capture the status of a simple command-line operation.

For example:

```
# Run a native application (e.g., ping)
ping localhost


# Check the last exit code
```

Write-Host "The exit code is: $LastExitCode"

If the ping is successful, $LastExitCode will be 0.

Integrating $LastExitCode

Imagine a section of our system monitoring script needs to perform a network diagnostic using the native ping utility. The goal is to ping a specific server, and if the ping fails, the script should log this failure.

```
# Ping a specific server
ping yourServerAddress -n 1


# Check if it was successful
if ($LastExitCode -ne 0) {
    Write-Host "Ping failed. Logging the failure."
    # Here, the code to log this failure would follow
}
```

Using $LastExitCode with Script Blocks

You can also employ $LastExitCode within script blocks to better manage flow control.

```
{
    ping yourServerAddress -n 1
    if ($LastExitCode -ne 0) { return $false }

    # Other checks
}
```

Chained Commands

In more sophisticated cases, you may chain several commands together. $LastExitCode can still help you, but be careful: it contains the exit code of the last command in the chain.

```
# Chain commands
ping localhost & netstat

# Exit code of the last command (netstat)
$LastExitCode
```

Logging with $LastExitCode

You should incorporate $LastExitCode into your main logging engine. When a job fails, you can note not just the failure but also the exit code, which provides useful context for troubleshooting.

```
# Hypothetical log entry structure
$logEntry = @{
   "Timestamp" = Get-Date
   "LastExitCode" = $LastExitCode
   "Event" = "DiskCheck"
}

# Log the data
$logEntry | ConvertTo-Json | Out-File -Append -Path "C:\Path\To\Log\File.log"
```

Troubleshooting and Decision-making

$LastExitCode may also influence decision-making. For example, if a backup process fails, the script might decide to halt further activities and send an alert, so immediate action can be taken.

```
# Execute a backup command
Backup-Utility

# Check exit code
if ($LastExitCode -ne 0) {
   # Send alert
```

```
    Send-Alert "Backup failed with exit code $LastExitCode."
    # Halt further script execution
    exit
}
```

As a flexible and essential component for strong, real-world monitoring solutions, $LastExitCode allows our system monitoring script to communicate without a hitch with native apps and external commands.

$MyInvocation Variable

It is time to delve into $MyInvocation within the framework of our continuing learning of system monitoring scripts. This is another automatic variable in PowerShell that stores information about the current command, script, or scope. It is excellent for debugging, logging, and developing more dynamic and responsive scripts. Given its role in getting metadata about the script or function it invokes, $MyInvocation can be useful in advanced monitoring solutions.

The $MyInvocation variable contains a plethora of information about the current command or script. When you call this variable from a function, script, or script block, it returns an object with properties that include information about the invocation environment. These attributes can include the script name, script line number, command used to execute the script, and much more.

$MyInvocation for Debugging and Logging

$MyInvocation can offer much-needed context about what part of the script is currently running, should an error or issue arise. Consider adding $MyInvocation properties to your logging functions to capture details like:

- Script Name: $MyInvocation.MyCommand.Name

- Line Number: $MyInvocation.ScriptLineNumber

- Invocation History: $MyInvocation.InvocationName

- Practical Use Cases in System Monitoring Script

Assume or consider that you have a function in your monitoring script that checks disk space. In this function, you can incorporate $MyInvocation to log relevant information:

```
function Check-DiskSpace {
    # Check disk space logic here

    $logEntry = @{
        "Function" = $MyInvocation.MyCommand.Name
        "Timestamp" = Get-Date
        "LineNumber" = $MyInvocation.ScriptLineNumber
        # Additional logging data
    }

    # Write to log
    $logEntry | ConvertTo-Json | Out-File -Append -Path "C:\Path\To\Log\File.log"
}
```

In this way, each log entry will include the function name (Check-DiskSpace) and the line number from which the log entry was made, providing an extra layer of information for debugging and auditing.

Dynamic Script Behavior

Another powerful way to use $MyInvocation is to create scripts that behave differently depending on how they are invoked. This is particularly helpful in system monitoring when certain checks or operations should only be conducted in specific scenarios. The $MyInvocation.Line property can reveal the exact line used to invoke the script or function, letting you dynamically adjust behavior.

For instance, consider that you want to skip a network check if the script is run with a -SkipNetworkCheck switch:

```
if ($MyInvocation.Line -notmatch "SkipNetworkCheck") {
    # Perform network check
} else {
    Write-Host "Skipping network check as per invocation."
```

}

Script Reflection

$MyInvocation can also help in script reflection, which is the script's ability to examine its own metadata. For example, if your monitoring script is modular and each module resides in its own file, $MyInvocation.MyCommand.Path can reveal the path to the module file. This is particularly useful if your script modules reside in different directories but are called into a main orchestrator script.

```
# Inside a script module
$modulePath = $MyInvocation.MyCommand.Path
```

With this approach, you can determine the location of each module programmatically and handle them accordingly, maybe even performing version checks or updating them dynamically. For even more detailed metadata, you can explore $MyInvocation.PSCommandPath, $MyInvocation.PSScriptRoot, and $MyInvocation.PSCommandDefinition among others, to get information about the script or function, its directory, or its definition.

$Args for Script Parameters

$Args in Monitoring Scripts

This $Args variable is another one that requires careful attention. This automated variable is used to handle script arguments that are not explicitly stated in a function or script's param block. It functions as an array to receive these "loose" or "unbound" arguments, making your script more versatile and adaptive. The $Args variable is effectively an array that holds all unbound arguments supplied to a script or function. For example, if your script is configured to take particular named parameters such as -Path or -Name, any additional parameters you supply that are not expressly specified will be caught by $Args.

Consider a variety of checks like disk, CPU, network, and so on; each with its own set of constraints. $Args allows you to give in a list of optional arguments that are only relevant for specific tests without having to explicitly define each one. This allows for greater flexibility in how checks can be conducted or set.

Sample Program: Passing Parameters

To understand this, let us add a function in our script that performs a CPU load check. Normally, this function might have named parameters for setting thresholds, but with $Args, you can provide additional information that is only sometimes relevant, like the processor core to focus the check on.

Given below is how it can be done:

```
function Check-CPU {
    param(
        [int]$Threshold
    )


    # Perform the CPU check logic here


    # Utilize $Args for additional, ad-hoc parameters
    if ($Args.Count -gt 0) {
        $CoreIndex = $Args[0]
        # Specific core monitoring logic here
    }


    # Create a log entry with optional $Args content
    $logData = @{
        "Function" = $MyInvocation.MyCommand.Name
        "Timestamp" = Get-Date
        "Threshold" = $Threshold
    }


    if ($Args.Count -gt 0) {
        $logData["CoreIndex"] = $CoreIndex
    }


    # Write to log
```

```
    $logData | ConvertTo-Json | Out-File -Append -Path "C:\Path\To\Log\File.log"
}
```

In the above sample program, the Check-CPU function uses a declared parameter $Threshold to specify a CPU usage level that should trigger an alert. However, it also uses $Args to capture an optional processor core index. This is particularly useful for servers with multiple processor cores where you may need to check CPU usage for a specific core. The script logs this information only if the $Args array is not empty, providing context in the logs.

Mixing $Args with Regular Parameters

You can use $Args alongside explicitly declared parameters. The key is that $Args only captures what is not already caught by the param block. For example, if you invoke the Check-CPU function as follows:

Check-CPU -Threshold 80 2

Here, 80 will be bound to the $Threshold parameter, and 2 will be captured by $Args, allowing for the extra functionality to monitor a specific core.

While $Args offers flexibility, it can also introduce ambiguity. Because $Args captures all unbound parameters, you must be cautious when passing in extra arguments. Without explicit naming, the sequence of these arguments matters, and it's easy to introduce errors.

For instance, if your function is expecting the first item in $Args to be a core index, but you pass in something else, that could lead to issues. Therefore, thorough validation of $Args contents is essential.

```
if ($Args.Count -gt 0) {
    $maybeCoreIndex = $Args[0]
    if ($maybeCoreIndex -is [int]) {
        # Valid core index, proceed
    } else {
        # Log an error or take other actions
    }
}
```

Your system monitoring script can accept many optional parameters with ease and adaptability if you use $Args. This allows your script to manage more arguments without being too complicated. It is especially beneficial for modular and developing scripts that must allow for extension. However, like with any powerful feature, $Args must be utilized with caution and a focus on validation to avoid potential hazards.

Summary

In this chapter, we looked at PowerShell's automatic variables, specifically how they might improve the usability and efficiency of a system monitoring script. Starting with $Error, we discovered its usefulness in recording exceptions and errors in a log, which is critical for troubleshooting. We saw how $Host and $Profile provide additional context by allowing modification based on the execution environment. These variables help to shape the behavior and output of scripts based on the host application, which is very valuable in system monitoring solutions that run in a variety of environments.

We also learned about the $Null variable, emphasizing its use in conditional checks and operations where the lack of a value is as important as its existence. Understanding how $Null interacts with other objects is critical for creating powerful PowerShell scripts. In contrast, $PSVersionTable provided information on the version of PowerShell being used, including compatibility and feature availability. This is critical in instances where scripts may execute on many systems using different PowerShell versions.

Shifting gears, we looked at $LastExitCode, which returns the exit code of the most recently executed application and provides a means for checking the success or failure of external actions within the script. It is especially important for system monitoring scripts that rely on third-party utilities for certain tests. Then came $MyInvocation, which provides metadata about the command being executed, allowing us to log additional information for easier auditing and debugging.

Finally, the $Args variable arose as a versatile mechanism for dealing with unbound script parameters, allowing for greater adaptability. We learnt how to use $Args in conjunction with clearly defined parameters to capture additional, ad-hoc arguments that may only be useful in certain circumstances. However, it was also highlighted that this flexibility comes at the expense of potential ambiguity, necessitating extensive validation to avoid errors. This chapter has taught you how to make the most of these automated variables, allowing your system monitoring scripts to be more effective, flexible and resilient.

Chapter 7: Debugging Techniques

Debugging Overview

Debugging is the systematic process of identifying and reducing the amount of bugs, or defects, in a computer program to ensure it operates as intended. Debugging is essentially investigative work. It's about determining why a piece of code isn't delivering the desired results. This could be for a variety of reasons, including flawed reasoning, misunderstood needs, or unanticipated inputs, to mention a few.

Before getting into debugging, you must verify that you understand the program's expected behavior. This includes understanding the program's needs and planned functionality. One of the most important aspects in debugging is being able to consistently reproduce the undesirable behavior. If you can't reproduce the bug, it's nearly impossible to know whether you've genuinely fixed it. For experts, this frequently entails developing a basic replication case—a simpler version of the software that nonetheless demonstrates the incorrect behavior. Beginners should take the time to stroll over the code, making sure they understand the flow and rationale. Professionals, on the other hand, may be familiar with the overall architecture but should review the specifics of the bug in question.

Most modern programming environments provide debugging tools. These tools enable you to pause execution (breakpoint), step through code one line at a time, inspect variable values, and much more. Professionals who are already familiar with these technologies may benefit from researching advanced features or updates. Beginners should prioritize being familiar with the basic debugging tool functionalities.

Also, sometimes the problem is not with the code itself, but with the environment in which it is executed. This may involve library versions, system configurations, or external services. Professionals that work with more complicated systems must be aware of environmental influences, particularly in distributed systems or microservices designs. Beginners, while dealing with basic setups, should be aware of this potential mistake. When you're too near to a problem, it can be difficult to perceive the solution. Explaining the problem to a coworker (or even an inanimate item, such as a rubber duck) might occasionally result in a startling realization. This technique, sometimes known as "rubber duck debugging," is effective for developers at all levels of their careers.

It is especially important for novices to realize that making mistakes is a natural part of the learning process. Instead than becoming upset or overwhelmed, see each bug as an opportunity to learn and improve. Professionals should view debugging as an essential component of software development—an opportunity to hone their skills and gain a deeper understanding of the system.

Write-Host Cmdlets

The Write-Host cmdlet is typically used to display information directly to the PowerShell console, allowing for personalized displays of messages, data, or other outputs. Unlike other cmdlets that send their output to the pipeline, Write-Host sends their output directly to the console/host.

Following are the key features of this cmdlet:

Colored Outputs
One of the standout features of Write-Host is its ability to produce colored text outputs, offering an effective way to highlight specific parts of a message.

For example:

Write-Host "This is a critical message!" -ForegroundColor Red

No Pipeline Pass
Information presented via Write-Host doesn't get passed down the PowerShell pipeline. This ensures that only the intended text gets displayed without any risk of it being processed by subsequent cmdlets in a pipeline.

Versatility
This cmdlet is highly flexible. Apart from strings, it can handle other objects, breaking them down and displaying their properties.

Imagine a system administration script that checks server health. During its run, Write-Host can be used to display intermediate statuses or instructions:

Write-Host "Checking server health..."
Server health check logic
Write-Host "Health check complete!" -ForegroundColor Green

Write-Error Cmdlet

While Write-Host is ideal for generating user-centric outputs, Write-Error is tailored for error handling. It generates a terminating or non-terminating error message to the console, allowing script developers to gracefully handle unexpected situations.

Following are the key features of this cmdlet:

Custom Error Messages
You can craft detailed error messages that provide valuable information about the nature and location of the problem. This aids significantly in debugging.

Non-Terminating
Unless specified, Write-Error produces non-terminating errors, meaning the script will continue to execute subsequent lines after encountering the error.

Error Category Specification
PowerShell classifies errors into different categories, like 'NotSpecified', 'InvalidOperation', or 'PermissionDenied'. Using Write-Error, you can specify which category your error belongs to.

Assume for a moment that the system monitoring script we discussed before checks the available disk space. If the available space falls below a specific threshold, it may be marked as an error.

```
$diskSpace = Get-DiskSpace # Hypothetical function
if ($diskSpace -lt 10) {
    Write-Error -Message "Disk space critically low!" -Category ResourceUnavailable
}
```

While both cmdlets deal with sending messages to the console, their core purposes differ:

- Write-Host is all about direct communication with the user. Its primary role is to display messages, data, or other outputs straight to the console in a format tailored for user consumption. Write-Error, on the other hand, is dedicated to error handling. It's about signaling problems or unexpected situations in the script's operation, allowing for both the developer and end-user to be informed of issues that need attention.

- If the intention is to give feedback, directions, or general information to the end-user, Write-Host is the go-to cmdlet. When the script encounters a situation where something goes amiss, or an unexpected condition is met, using Write-Error is appropriate. It ensures that the problem is logged, and necessary actions can be taken.

- If you're generating logs or reports that will later be analyzed, Write-Error is more suitable for logging anomalies, while Write-Host can be employed for general informational messages.

Sample Program: Using Write-Host and Write-Error

Our current system monitoring script checks several components, including server uptime, disk space, CPU use, and RAM usage. We will expand upon this script for demonstration.

Utilizing Write-Host for Feedback and Status

A fundamental aspect of system monitoring is to provide real-time feedback to users. Write-Host serves this purpose by displaying custom messages directly on the console.

```
$uptime = Get-Uptime # Hypothetical function that returns server uptime in hours


# Displaying initial status
Write-Host "Initiating server uptime check..."


if ($uptime -ge 24) {
    Write-Host "Server has been running for over 24 hours." -ForegroundColor Yellow
} else {
    Write-Host "Server uptime is under 24 hours." -ForegroundColor Green
}
```

Here, Write-Host not only communicates the beginning of the check but also gives feedback based on the result. The color coding further emphasizes the message's importance.

Using Write-Error for Disk Space Alerts

If disk space goes below a threshold, it's imperative to alert the user. Write-Error shines in such scenarios by generating non-terminating errors.

```
$diskSpace = Get-DiskSpace # Hypothetical function that fetches available disk space in GB


# Informing user about the check
```

```
Write-Host "Analyzing available disk space..."

if ($diskSpace -lt 10) {
    Write-Error -Message "CRITICAL: Disk space is below 10GB!" -Category ResourceUnavailable
} else {
    Write-Host "Disk space is adequate." -ForegroundColor Green
}
```

Upon detecting low disk space, Write-Error creates an error message that is both eye-catching and informative, making it hard for users to overlook.

Combining Write-Host and Write-Error for CPU Monitoring

Both cmdlets can be employed together for a comprehensive monitoring solution.

```
cpuUsage = Get-CpuUsage # Hypothetical function that returns CPU usage percentage

Write-Host "Starting CPU usage assessment..."

if ($cpuUsage -ge 90) {
    Write-Error -Message "ALERT: CPU usage is above 90%!" -Category Performance
    Write-Host "Please consider checking running processes or restarting the system." -ForegroundColor Red
} elseif ($cpuUsage -ge 75) {
    Write-Host "WARNING: CPU usage is between 75% and 90%." -ForegroundColor Yellow
} else {
    Write-Host "CPU usage is under control." -ForegroundColor Green
}
```

In this above code, Write-Host and Write-Error work in tandem. If CPU usage is critically high,

Write-Error highlights the issue, while Write-Host provides additional suggestions or information.

Memory Monitoring with Clear Communication

Efficient communication ensures that users are well-informed about potential issues.

```
$ramUsage = Get-RamUsage # Hypothetical function that fetches RAM usage percentage

Write-Host "Evaluating RAM consumption..."

if ($ramUsage -ge 85) {
    Write-Error -Message "WARNING: RAM usage exceeds 85%!" -Category Performance
    Write-Host "Consider closing unnecessary applications to free up memory." -ForegroundColor Yellow
} else {
    Write-Host "RAM usage is within optimal limits." -ForegroundColor Green
}
```

The combination of Write-Error and Write-Host ensures that users receive clear messages about potential issues and actionable steps.

Key Learnings

- Feedback is Paramount: Consistent feedback, provided by Write-Host, ensures users are kept in the loop about the script's progress and findings.

- Error Visibility: Write-Error ensures that critical issues don't go unnoticed. Its output is distinct and demands attention.

- Harmony in Usage: While each cmdlet has its strengths, combining them in the right manner makes scripts more user-friendly and efficient.

- Enhanced User Experience: Through thoughtful scripting and the strategic use of these cmdlets, you can drastically enhance user experience, making scripts both informative and actionable.

Using Breakpoints for Effective Debugging

Overview

When scripts become more complicated, unanticipated behaviors may occur, demanding extensive examination. In these situations, PowerShell's debugging tool, breakpoints, is really useful. We shall look at breakpoints and how to use them in practice.

Breakpoints are designated points in a script where execution is briefly interrupted, allowing the debugger to check the current state of the program, variables, or other components. Once halted, the script can be stepped through line by line to see variable values and comprehend the flow.

Types of Breakpoints:

1. Line Breakpoints: The most common type. Execution stops before the designated line runs.

2. Variable Breakpoints: Execution halts when a specific variable is accessed or modified.

3. Command Breakpoints: Stops when a particular command or function is about to be executed.

Setting Breakpoints

In PowerShell, the Set-PSBreakpoint cmdlet (often abbreviated as sbp) is used to create breakpoints.

Example 1: Line Breakpoint

To set a breakpoint on a specific line of a script:

Set-PSBreakpoint -Script <ScriptPath> -Line <LineNumber>

For instance, given our system monitoring script, if you wanted to stop execution on line 10:

Set-PSBreakpoint -Script 'C:\path\to\system-monitor.ps1' -Line 10

Example 2: Variable Breakpoint

To pause execution when a particular variable is modified:

Set-PSBreakpoint -Script <ScriptPath> -Variable <VariableName>

If you wish to halt whenever the $cpuUsage variable in our system monitoring script is modified:

Set-PSBreakpoint -Script 'C:\path\to\system-monitor.ps1' -Variable cpuUsage

Example 3: Command Breakpoint

To create a breakpoint on a specific command or function:

Set-PSBreakpoint -Script <ScriptPath> -Command <CommandOrFunctionName>

If the system monitoring script contains a function called CheckNetwork, and you wish to stop right before it's executed:

Set-PSBreakpoint -Script 'C:\path\to\system-monitor.ps1' -Command CheckNetwork

Working with Breakpoints During Debugging

After setting breakpoints, when you run your script and it hits a breakpoint, the execution will pause. In this halted state:

- Use the s key to "step into" functions or scripts, allowing you to dive deeper into specific areas of your code.

- The v key allows you to "step over" lines, meaning you can progress through your script without diving into functions or scripts.

- Pressing c will "continue" execution until the next breakpoint or the script's end.

- q will stop debugging and terminate the script.

Additionally, while stopped at a breakpoint, you can inspect variable values simply by typing their names.

Managing Breakpoints

- Listing Breakpoints: Use Get-PSBreakpoint to see all breakpoints in your session. It'll display line numbers, script names, and other crucial details.

- Removing Breakpoints: The Remove-PSBreakpoint cmdlet (or rbp) allows for breakpoint deletion. You can delete specific breakpoints or all at once.

- Enabling and Disabling: Instead of removing a breakpoint, you might want to temporarily disable it. Use Enable-PSBreakpoint and Disable-PSBreakpoint accordingly.

Consider the following scenario:
Our system monitoring script has expanded substantially, and someone suspects that the CheckNetwork function isn't functioning properly.

Now, to debug, you set a command breakpoint on CheckNetwork:

Set-PSBreakpoint -Script 'C:\path\to\system-monitor.ps1' -Command CheckNetwork

Run the script. Once the CheckNetwork function is about to execute, the script will halt, allowing you to step into the function with the s key.

As you navigate through the function, monitor variables to see if they hold expected values. If $networkStatus is a variable within that function, simply type its name to inspect its current value. If you encounter any loops or other functions within CheckNetwork that you don't wish to step into, use the v key to step over.

Once you've ascertained the issue or need to check another part of your script, press c to continue execution or q to quit.

Debugging in Remote Sessions

Debugging is already a powerful tool when you're dealing with scripts on your local machine. But what if you need to troubleshoot scripts running on a different server or device? This is where the concept of debugging in remote sessions comes into play. We shall break down this essential skill.

Debugging in a remote session implies that you're investigating and solving script issues on a remote machine, from your local environment. With PowerShell, this is achieved using remote sessions or "PSSessions," which are established through the WS-Management protocol.

Remote debugging is invaluable for multiple reasons:

- Environment-specific issues: Sometimes, scripts run perfectly on one machine but falter on another due to environmental differences.

- Secure Environment: You might not want or have the permission to move certain scripts out of a secured environment, making remote debugging the only viable option.

- Convenience: Logging into another machine can be time-consuming or might require additional setup. Remote debugging bypasses this need, letting you address issues directly.

Establishing Remote Session

Before diving into remote debugging, it's imperative to understand how to initiate a remote session. PowerShell offers the New-PSSession cmdlet to create these:

$session = New-PSSession -ComputerName 'RemoteServerName'

Here, $session holds the session details, allowing you to enter, manage, and exit the session as needed.

Enter and Exit Remote Session

Once a session is initiated, you can enter it using Enter-PSSession and the session variable:

Enter-PSSession -Session $session

When inside, your prompt changes, indicating you're now operating on the remote machine. To exit, simply type exit.

Enable Remote Debugging

By default, PowerShell doesn't allow remote debugging for security reasons. To enable it, you have to modify the PSRemotingTransportVersion parameter:

On your local machine, set:

$DebugPreference = 'RemoteSigned'

On the remote machine, set:

Set-Item WSMan:\localhost\Shell\AllowRemoteShellAccess $true

This modification ensures that remote sessions can transfer debugging information back and forth.

Executing and Debugging Remotely

Suppose this script resides on a remote server and, for some reason, isn't producing the expected results.

Start by copying the script to the remote session:

Copy-Item -Path 'C:\path\to\system-monitor.ps1' -Destination 'C:\remote\path' -ToSession $session

Now, enter the remote session:

Enter-PSSession -Session $session

Navigate to the directory where you copied the script:

cd C:\remote\path

Set a breakpoint in the script, say, on line 10:

Set-PSBreakpoint -Script .\system-monitor.ps1 -Line 10

Run the script:

.\system-monitor.ps1

Execution will halt when it hits the breakpoint, just as it would on your local machine. Now, you can inspect variables, step through code, and use all the debugging techniques learned earlier, but all of it's happening on the remote server!

Closing the Loop

Once done with debugging, it's vital to exit the remote session and, if needed, close it:

```
exit
Remove-PSSession -Session $session
```

This ensures that the connection is gracefully terminated, freeing up resources.

You can debug without a hitch on the remote system if you set up a remote session, enable remote debugging, and transfer scripts. This strategy not only provides convenience, but it also solves environmental challenges directly in their natural habitat.

Debugging Tools

The Integrated Scripting Environment (ISE) is a versatile scripting workbench that includes a variety of tools to make your life easier, particularly when debugging. Among the many capabilities available, the ISE Debugger and the Variables Pane stand out as particularly useful for debugging.

We need to learn how to use these tools well, so let us take the time to study them thoroughly.

ISE Debugger

The ISE Debugger is designed to pause the execution of your script, allowing you to inspect its state, control its execution, and interact with the script in real-time.

Features and Functionalities

- Breakpoints: These are specific points in your code where you instruct the debugger to pause execution. This pause lets you inspect the current state, including variable values, the call stack, and the command history.

- Step Through Execution: Once paused, you can control how the script continues. You can step line by line, delve into functions, or run until the next breakpoint.

- Runtime State Inspection: Examine variable values, modify them, or even run new commands within the script's environment.

Using ISE Debugger

- Setting Breakpoints: In the ISE Editor, simply click on the left margin next to a line of code. A red dot appears, indicating a breakpoint. You can also right-click and choose 'Toggle Breakpoint'.

- Running the Script: Execute your script as usual. Execution will halt at breakpoints, letting you examine the environment.

- Controlling Execution: On the toolbar or through hotkeys:

- F10 / 'Step Over': Execute the current line and pause on the next one.

- F11 / 'Step Into': If the current line is a function or script, delve into it and pause on its first line. If not, it behaves like 'Step Over'.

- Shift + F11 / 'Step Out': If inside a function or script, run until it completes and then pause.

- F5 / 'Continue': Resume regular execution until the next breakpoint.

Variables Pane

The Variables pane in the ISE provides a live, interactive view of all the variables currently in your script's environment. It's invaluable for understanding the data your script is working with.

Features and Functionalities
- Variable Listing: See all variables, their types, and current values.

- Scope Filtering: Examine variables in specific scopes, be it the global scope, script scope, or within a particular function.

- Interactive Modification: Change variable values on the fly, aiding in what-if scenarios or rectifying undesired states.

Using Variables Pane
- Accessing the Pane: By default, the Variables pane is located on the lower side of the ISE. If not visible, enable it from the 'View' menu.

- Inspecting Variables: All active variables are listed with their current values. Clicking on a variable reveals more details, including its type.

- Modifying Variables: Double-click on a variable's value to edit it. This change is reflected immediately in the script's environment.

Sample Program: Using ISE Debugger and Variables Pane

We shall show these capabilities in action by utilizing our script for system monitoring.

For ISE Debugger
1. Open the system monitoring script in ISE.

2. Set a breakpoint on a line, say where the script checks if a server is online.
3. Run the script. Execution will pause at our breakpoint.
4. Now, step through the code using F10 or F11. Observe how you can control the flow, delve into functions, and inspect the runtime environment.
5. Feel free to modify the script, add more breakpoints, and explore the depth of the ISE Debugger's capabilities.

For Variables Pane
1. With our script still paused from above (or run it till a breakpoint if not), look at the Variables pane.
2. Notice variables related to server status, their values, and perhaps other temporary variables.
3. Change a variable's value. For instance, if you have a variable $serverStatus with a value "Offline", change it to "Online".
4. Continue the script execution. Observe how this change affects the script's behavior.

You may quickly identify problems, understand their origins, and design remedies by pausing the script, inspecting its surroundings, changing its state, and managing its execution. Everyone from PowerShell newbies attempting to better understand their scripts to seasoned pros searching for obscure flaws can benefit from the ISE Debugger and Variables Pane.

Decoding Stack Traces

Understanding Stack Trace

A stack trace, at its core, is a report detailing the execution path a program took leading up to a specific point, typically an error or exception. Think of it as the breadcrumb trail left behind by the program, marking its journey through different functions or methods.

Every time a function is called in a program, details of that function, including where it was called from and its local variables, are pushed onto the call stack. If that function, in turn, calls another, details of this second function are added to the stack on top of the first. This process continues with each nested function call. When an error occurs, or when specifically requested, this stack can be 'traced' from the top (the point of error or current function) down to the very first function that was called, providing a snapshot of the execution sequence.

Components of a Stack Trace
- Function/Method Name: Specifies which function or method was executing.

- File Name & Path: Tells us in which file the error occurred.

- Line Number: Pinpoints the exact line within the file where things went awry.

- Caller Information: Reveals which function or method called the current one.

- Exception Message (if applicable): Provides a brief description of the error.

Benefits of Analyzing Stack Trace
- Rather than sifting through hundreds of lines of code, the stack trace guides you directly to the problematic spot.

- Gives insight into the sequence of function calls, aiding in comprehension of the program's flow.

- Speeds up the debugging process by providing essential details at a glance.

Sample Program: Analyzing Stack Traces

Now that we know how to debug our system monitoring script, let us return to it and examine its stack trace in detail. Consider the following scenario: our script is expected to read a file containing a list of server names and then check their status. However, we provided an incorrect path to the file, resulting in a failure.

```
function CheckServerStatus($serverName) {
    # Simulated function to check server status
    # ...
}


function LoadServersFromFile($filePath) {
    if (-not (Test-Path $filePath)) {
        throw "File not found: $filePath"
    }
    # Read the file and return server names
    # ...
}
```

```
try {
  $servers = LoadServersFromFile("wrong/path/to/servers.txt")
  foreach ($server in $servers) {
    CheckServerStatus($server)
  }
} catch {
  Write-Error $_.Exception.ToString()
  Write-Error $_.Exception.StackTrace
}
```

Upon execution, the script will fail when attempting to load the server names. This will produce an exception with a stack trace that might look something like:

File not found: wrong/path/to/servers.txt
   at LoadServersFromFile in C:\path\to\script.ps1:line 8
   at <ScriptBlock> in C:\path\to\script.ps1:line 20

Decoding the Trace

- The error message is clear: "File not found."

- The location of the error is within the LoadServersFromFile function.

- The erroneous line is line 8 of the script located at C:\path\to\script.ps1.

- The call to LoadServersFromFile was made from a script block, specifically from line 20.

This trace provides an accurate view of where and why the issue occurred. In this situation, we'd understand that we need to double-check the file path sent to the LoadServersFromFile function. To summarize, stack traces, while initially daunting, are an extremely useful tool for any developer or scripter. Once you understand their structure and meaning, you'll discover that these traces, far from being a source of confusion, are excellent friends in your debugging efforts.

Summary

This chapter explains the essence of PowerShell debugging, shining light on its details and importance. Debugging is similar to detective work, requiring rigorous attention to find and correct flaws or inefficiencies in scripts. A key takeaway was that debugging is more than just problem resolution; it is also about optimizing code to make it more effective and efficient. When we looked into the tools and approaches, we learned about cmdlets like Write-Host and Write-Error. While Write-Host is useful for presenting information directly to the terminal, Write-Error is critical when generating non-terminating problems. These technologies, when used correctly in our system monitoring script example, improved user feedback and error reporting, making the script more usable and manageable.

Breakpoints emerged as an effective debugging feature, allowing script execution to be interrupted at certain points. Breakpoints can be used to investigate variable values, control flow, and script behavior, allowing for more granular code analysis. This is especially useful when dealing with complex scripts with possible faults hidden deep inside the code levels. On the other hand, remote session debugging was another sophisticated concept investigated. It broadens the debugging horizon by allowing developers to remotely start, monitor, and debug scripts, which is essential for controlling and troubleshooting scripts on remote servers or devices.

We also explored PowerShell ISE's integrated environment, focusing on two essential debugging tools: the Command Add-on and the Debugging Console. Both tools, each with its own set of features, provide developers with a more visual and interactive debugging experience. Finally, the mystery of stack traces was unraveled. Stack traces, while scary at first appearance, are actually a roadmap to the source of an issue. Understanding its components, from the function or method name to the specific line number of the problem, allows one to quickly detect and correct errors.

Overall, this chapter stressed that debugging is a proactive method that, when integrated into the development process, results in robust and efficient scripts, rather than a reactive one performed after an error is detected.

Chapter 8: Working with While Loops

Essence of While Loops

Programming is more than just sending instructions to a machine; it is also about organizing these instructions in ways that are efficient, adaptive, and intuitive. This orchestration relies heavily on control structures like loops. Among the several looping techniques in PowerShell, the 'While' loop stands out as both fundamental and necessary. Its simplicity belies its capability, and for PowerShell developers, mastering it is analogous to a musician learning scales: simple yet essential.

A 'While' loop executes a block of code as long as a certain condition is true. It checks the condition before performing the loop's body. If the condition returns true, the loop's body is run. This cycle continues until the condition becomes false.

```
while (condition)
{
    # Code to execute while the condition is true
}
```

The 'While' loop serves primarily as a flow control mechanism. Certain processes in programming frequently require repeating, either for a predetermined number of times or until a specific state is obtained. 'While' loops are ideal for the latter, making them useful for activities such as expecting user input, monitoring system conditions, and retrying procedures.

Consider the following scenario: a PowerShell script should continue to check if a specific file exists on a system and only proceed if it does. Using a 'While' loop, the script can efficiently poll for the file without moving forward, guaranteeing that subsequent file-dependent operations do not fail. Also, the 'While' loop is extremely flexible. It can be used in a wide range of applications, from simple counting to more complicated processes involving arrays or system checks. The loop's condition may be a simple comparison, a complicated logical condition, or even function calls that yield a boolean value. This means that a developer can use the 'While' loop in almost any circumstance where repeated actions based on a condition are required.

A well-designed 'While' loop can be greatly optimized to ensure that resources are used efficiently. For example, in circumstances where processes may be resource-intensive, the loop can be designed to include sleep intervals, ensuring that the system is not overwhelmed.

A PowerShell developer's arsenal also includes 'While' loops as a protective technique. They act as safety nets, ensuring that scripts do not run when they should. Consider a script designed to manage database entries. A 'While' loop can continuously monitor the database's health or availability, guaranteeing that operations do not proceed if the database is offline and thereby preventing potential data corruption.

In monitoring circumstances when a script needs to maintain track of system metrics or application statuses, 'While' loops can poll and check these metrics on a regular basis, taking actions such as issuing alarms or restarting services as needed. In the huge ocean of programming, 'while' loops may appear as simple raindrops. Nonetheless, their depth and potential are immense. For a PowerShell developer, they are more than simply tools; they are essential building blocks for creating dynamic, resilient, and efficient scripts.

Syntax and Structure

Basic Syntax

The 'While' loop has a straightforward syntax, but understanding its structure and the different ways it can be employed is crucial for harnessing its full potential. The foundational structure of a 'While' loop is deceptively simple as below:

```
while (condition)
{
    # Code to be executed as long as the condition is true
}
```

Here, "condition" is a statement that returns a boolean value: either $true or $false. The loop will continuously execute the enclosed code block as long as the condition remains true.

For example, we shall start with a basic counter:

```
$count = 1
while ($count -le 5)
{
    Write-Output "Current count: $count"
    $count++
}
```

In the above snippet, the script initializes a $count variable with a value of 1. The 'While' loop then checks if $count is less than or equal to 5. If true, it outputs the current count and then increments it by 1. This continues until $count exceeds 5, at which point the loop terminates.

Compound Conditions

The 'While' loop isn't limited to single conditions. You can combine multiple conditions using logical operators like -and, -or, and -not.

Suppose you want to monitor a system process and also check that a certain time threshold hasn't been exceeded:

```
$startTime = Get-Date
while ((Get-Process -Name "Notepad" -ErrorAction SilentlyContinue) -and ((Get-Date) - $startTime).Minutes -lt 10))
{
    Write-Output "Notepad is still running."
    Start-Sleep -Seconds 30
}
```

Here, the 'While' loop checks two conditions: whether the Notepad process is running and if less than 10 minutes have passed since the script started. It will keep checking every 30 seconds for up to 10 minutes or until Notepad is closed.

Do-While

The 'Do-While' loop is a version of the 'While' loop available in PowerShell. This structure ensures that the code block is executed at least once, regardless of the original state of the condition.

```
do
{
    # Code to be executed
}
while (condition)
```

For example, if you're prompting a user for input and want to ensure they provide a valid response, a 'Do-While' loop can be useful:

```
do
{
    $input = Read-Host "Please enter a number greater than 10"
}
while ($input -le 10)
```

In this scenario, the script will keep prompting the user until they enter a number greater than 10.

$? Variable

To determine whether the previous command was successful, PowerShell uses the $? automatic variable. It can be used in a 'While' loop to keep a loop running as long as previous commands are executed successfully.

Consider a scenario where you want to copy files, but only as long as no errors occur:

```
$files = Get-ChildItem -Path "C:\SourceFolder"
foreach ($file in $files)
{
    Copy-Item -Path $file.FullName -Destination "D:\DestinationFolder"
    while ($?)
    {
        # Perhaps log the successful copy or perform another related action
        break
    }
}
```

In the above snippet, the 'While' loop will check the success of the Copy-Item command for each file. If it succeeds, it can log the success or execute additional commands.

Nesting 'While' Loops

'While' loops can be nested to provide more complicated flow control. For example, suppose you're monitoring two distinct resources:

```
while (Check-ResourceA)
{
    while (Check-ResourceB)
    {
        # Actions to perform when both ResourceA and ResourceB meet certain conditions
        Start-Sleep -Seconds 5
    }
    Start-Sleep -Seconds 10
}
```

Here, the script checks Check-ResourceA. If it returns true, it then checks Check-ResourceB. Actions are performed when both conditions are met, with different sleep intervals depending on the loop level.

Infinite Loops and Safe Exits

A word of caution: The flexibility of 'While' loops also means it's possible to create infinite loops if the conditions are never met. This is especially true if the logic within the loop does not have mechanisms to alter the condition being checked.

For example:

```
while ($true)
{
    $response = Read-Host "Do you want to exit? (yes/no)"
    if ($response -eq "yes")
    {
        break
    }
    Write-Output "Continuing the loop!"
}
```

Here, the loop will continuously prompt the user if they want to exit. Only if they enter "yes" will the loop terminate, thanks to the break statement. The break statement is a powerful ally inside loops, allowing for immediate termination.

Sample Program: Using While Loops for System Monitoring

Think back on the example we used for system monitoring. We can use a 'While' loop to repeatedly check the system's resources until we hit a specific threshold.

For example, we want to monitor CPU usage and alert when it's below a threshold for a sustained period:

```
$lowCount = 0

while ($lowCount -lt 5)
{
   $cpuUsage = Get-WmiObject win32_processor | Measure-Object -Property LoadPercentage -Average | Select-Object -ExpandProperty Average
   if ($cpuUsage -lt 20)
   {
     $lowCount++
     Write-Output "Low CPU usage detected: $cpuUsage%. Count: $lowCount"
   }
   else
   {
     $lowCount = 0
   }
   Start-Sleep -Seconds 30
}

Write-Output "CPU usage remained low for a consistent period!"
```

This script checks CPU usage every 30 seconds. If the usage is below 20% for 5 consecutive checks (or 2.5 minutes), it alerts the user.

Retry Mechanisms

'While' loops are especially handy when building retry mechanisms. If a particular operation fails, the loop can retry it until either it succeeds or a maximum retry count is reached.

Consider a scenario where we're trying to establish a network connection:

```
$retryCount = 0
$maxRetries = 5


while (!(Test-Connection -ComputerName "ServerName" -Count 1 -Quiet) -and ($retryCount -lt $maxRetries))
{
   $retryCount++
   Write-Output "Failed to connect. Attempt $retryCount of $maxRetries."
   Start-Sleep -Seconds 10
}
```

In this case, if the initial connection to "ServerName" fails, the script will attempt to reconnect up to 5 times, waiting 10 seconds between each try.

Continue Statement

PowerShell 'While' loops can benefit from the continue statement, which compels the next iteration of the loop to begin while bypassing any code that follows it.

For example:

```
$count = 0
while ($count -lt 10)
{
   $count++
   if ($count % 2 -ne 0)
```

```
    {
        continue
    }
    Write-Output "Even number: $count"
}
```

This script prints out even numbers between 1 and 10. When an odd number is encountered, the continue statement triggers the next iteration of the loop, skipping the Write-Output command.

Put simply, the 'While' loop is one of PowerShell's most flexible constructs. Its versatility allows it to be used in a variety of contexts, from simple counting tasks to complex system checks and retries.

Error Handling in While Loops

Possibility of Errors

There is no denying the versatility and adaptability of PowerShell's 'While' loops. However, enormous power carries the risk of error. These failures can be caused by the logic utilized inside the loop, resources accessible by the code within the loop, or other unanticipated circumstances.

Infinite Loops

A common mistake with 'While' loops is unintentionally creating an infinite loop. This can be due to a condition that is never met or an internal logic that fails to change the loop's control variable.

Resource Exhaustion

If a 'While' loop continuously accesses a system resource (like querying a database or a remote server), it might lead to resource exhaustion or even system failures.

External Dependencies

A 'While' loop relying on external resources, like network services or files, is vulnerable to errors if those resources become unavailable.

Managing Errors

The try, catch, and finally constructs in PowerShell provide a robust framework for error handling as below:

Try-Catch Block

The try block contains the code that might throw an error, while the catch block contains the code that will execute if an error is thrown. For example, consider we want to fetch a remote resource:

```
$retryCount = 0
$maxRetries = 5

while ($retryCount -lt $maxRetries)
{
   try
   {
      # Attempting to fetch a remote resource
      $resource = Invoke-WebRequest -Uri "http://remote.server/resource"
      if ($resource.StatusCode -eq 200) { break }  # Exit loop if successful
   }
   catch
   {
      Write-Output "Error encountered: $_.Exception.Message"
      $retryCount++
      Start-Sleep -Seconds 5
   }
}
```

In the above snippet, if there is an error fetching the remote resource, the catch block will log the error message and then wait for 5 seconds before the next attempt.

Finally Block

The finally block contains the code that will always execute after the try or catch block, regardless of whether there was an error. This is useful for cleanup activities.

For example:

```
$count = 0
while ($count -lt 5)
{
   try
   {
      # Some code that might produce an error
      $result = 10 / $count
   }
   catch
   {
      Write-Output "Error: Division by zero."
   }
   finally
   {
      $count++
   }
}
```

Here, even if the code inside the try block fails, the finally block ensures the $count variable is incremented, preventing a possible infinite loop.

Specific Errors

You can target specific errors by catching particular exception types. This allows you to handle different errors in unique ways.

For example:

```
try
{
   # Some code
}
```

```
catch [System.Net.WebException]
{
    Write-Output "Network error encountered."
}
catch
{
    Write-Output "General error encountered."
}
```

In this setup, network-related errors are caught by the first catch block, while all other errors are caught by the second.

Controlling Error Output

For custom error messages or controlling the output of errors within your loop, Write-Error is your tool. It lets you display error messages without breaking the script.

For example:

```
while ($true)
{
    $response = Read-Host "Enter a number"
    if ($response -notmatch '^\d+$')
    {
        Write-Error "Please enter a valid number!"
        continue
    }
    # Further processing
}
```

In this script, if a user enters an invalid input, a custom error message is displayed, prompting them to enter a number. The loop then continues to the next iteration without breaking.

Debugging While Loops

The use of PowerShell's 'While' loops efficiently is crucial for troubleshooting. Misbehaving loops can be difficult to diagnose because of their subtle nature, but they can have significant consequences, such as running indefinitely or depleting resources.

Identifying the Problem

Infinite Loop Diagnosis

An infinite loop is a common issue. It occurs when the loop's condition never evaluates to false. To diagnose, insert logging statements at the beginning and end of your loop. This can be done using Write-Host with a distinguishable message:

```
$count = 0
while ($count -lt 5)
{
    Write-Host "Loop starting iteration $count"
    # ... Loop Body ...
    Write-Host "Loop completed iteration $count"
    $count++
}
```

By monitoring the output, you can quickly gauge if your loop is iterating as expected or running indefinitely.

Conditional Check

Often, a logical error in the loop's condition might be the culprit. Carefully review the conditional expression. Ensure variables involved in the condition are being modified appropriately within the loop.

Interactive Debugging with Set-PSBreakpoint

Set-PSBreakpoint is particularly handy for 'While' loops. You can set a breakpoint at a specific line, and when execution reaches that line, the script pauses, allowing you to inspect variables and the environment.

For instance, in our example:

```
$index = 1
while ($index -le 10)
{
    # Fetch some system data
    $data = Get-Process
    $index++
}
```

If we want to inspect the $data variable during each iteration, we can set a breakpoint:

```
Set-PSBreakpoint -Script 'path_to_script.ps1' -Line line_number
```

Replace path_to_script.ps1 with the path to your script and line_number with the line where $data is populated.

Inspecting Variables

A crucial aspect of debugging is observing variable values. When the script is paused at a breakpoint, use the Get-Variable cmdlet to inspect any variable's value:

```
Get-Variable data
```

This cmdlet fetches the value of $data, giving insights into its content during each iteration.

Log Verbosely

Your script should include logging that is especially detailed. Use Write-Verbose to record precise messages about what your loop is doing. When debugging, execute the script with the -Verbose option to observe these messages.

```
$count = 0
while ($count -lt 5)
{
    Write-Verbose "Fetching system data..."
```

```
    # Fetch some system data
    $data = Get-Process
    Write-Verbose "Data fetched for iteration $count"
    $count++
}
```

When executed with the -Verbose option, detailed insights are provided, which helps with debugging.

Do-While and Do-Until Loops

The ability to execute a section of code numerous times in response to a condition is made available to developers by looping constructs such as the While loop. But there are other options besides While. The Do-While and Do-Until loops are two more loop constructions that provide significant benefits in specific scenarios.

Do-While Loop

The Do-While loop in PowerShell functions similarly to the regular While loop but with one major difference: the condition is evaluated after the loop's code block is executed, not before. This guarantees that the loop's code block is executed at least once, regardless of the condition.

Following is the syntax:

```
Do
{
   # Code block
}
While (condition)
```

Do-Until Loop

PowerShell doesn't have a built-in Do-Until loop like some other languages. However, it can be simulated using the Do-While loop by inverting the condition. The primary purpose of the Do-Until construct is to keep executing the loop's code block until a certain condition becomes true.

Following is the simulated syntax:

```
Do
{
  # Code block
}
While (-not condition)
```

The foremost advantage of these loops is their guarantee that the code block within the loop executes at least once. There might be situations where it's essential to execute the code block regardless of whether the condition is met initially. For instance, in our system monitoring script, if we want to capture the system's state at least once and then continue capturing based on some criteria, a Do-While loop would be suitable.

Sometimes, using a Do-While or Do-Until loop can make the intent of the code clearer. If the logic demands that a task be executed and then a condition checked, using these loops portrays this sequence more transparently.

Using in System Monitoring Script

Think back to the system monitoring example from before. If we wish to verify a system's health, capture the initial data, and then continue monitoring depending on specified criteria, a Do-While is appropriate:

```
Do
{
    $systemData = Get-SystemData # This is a hypothetical cmdlet for demonstration
    Log-Data $systemData # Again, a hypothetical cmdlet to log data

    # Wait for a specified interval before the next check
    Start-Sleep -Seconds 10
}
While ($systemData.HealthStatus -ne "Critical")
```

Here, the system's data is captured and logged at least once. The loop then continues monitoring until the system's health status becomes "Critical."

Combine Do-While and Do-Until Together

Foundation of Nested Looping

When one loop is positioned inside another, we call this a nested loop. The inner loop completes its entire cycle for every single cycle of the outer loop. This structure is used when a specific sequence of tasks must be repeated within another sequence.

Combining Do-While and Do-Until allows you to harness the strengths of both loop types. The Do-While loop guarantees that a block of code is executed at least once before checking its condition, while the Do-Until approach (simulated with Do-While) focuses on executing a block until a certain condition becomes true.

Sample Program: Exploit Nested Looping

Come back to the example of system monitoring. Assume our purpose is to continuously monitor the system, collect data at regular intervals, and then execute a certain operation until a secondary condition is met.

And the situation is as below:
- Monitor the system continuously until a 'shutdown' signal is detected.
- Within each monitoring cycle, attempt to establish a connection to a secondary system. Retry connecting until successful, but no more than five attempts per cycle.

Following is how you can script it:

```
$shutdownDetected = $false

Do
{
    # Capture primary system status
    $systemStatus = Get-SystemStatus # Hypothetical cmdlet to get system status

    if($systemStatus -eq 'shutdown')
    {
```

```powershell
        $shutdownDetected = $true
    }
    else
    {
        $connectionAttempts = 0
        $connectionEstablished = $false

        Do
        {
            $connectionStatus = Connect-SecondarySystem # Hypothetical cmdlet to establish a connection
            $connectionAttempts++

            if($connectionStatus -eq 'connected')
            {
                $connectionEstablished = $true
            }
            else
            {
                Write-Warning "Connection attempt $connectionAttempts failed."
                Start-Sleep -Seconds 5 # Wait for 5 seconds before retrying
            }
        }
        While (-not $connectionEstablished -and $connectionAttempts -lt 5)

        if($connectionEstablished)
        {
            # Perform tasks with the secondary system
            Execute-Tasks # Hypothetical cmdlet
```

```
        }
        else
        {
            Write-Error "Failed to establish connection after 5 attempts."
        }

        # Primary system monitoring sleep interval
        Start-Sleep -Seconds 60
    }
}
While (-not $shutdownDetected)
```

The outer Do-While loop checks the primary system's status continuously until a shutdown signal is detected. Inside this loop, a nested Do-Until loop (simulated with Do-While) attempts to establish a connection to the secondary system. This inner loop continues trying to connect until either a successful connection is made or the number of attempts reaches five.

In the above sample program, the script effectively sets up two monitoring conditions: one for the overall system status and another for secondary system connection attempts within each monitoring cycle.

Observations
- Nesting loops provides the flexibility to manage multiple repetitive tasks with varied conditions.
- Combining different loop types lets you exploit the specific advantages of each, offering nuanced control over the script's flow.
- As with any nested loop, it's crucial to have clear exit conditions to prevent potential infinite loops. Both the inner and outer loops should have conditions that will eventually be met.
- Properly indenting nested loops and providing informative comments can greatly enhance readability. This clarity is essential, especially as scripts become more complex.
- Using Do-While in conjunction with Do-Until offers the ability to guarantee that a task is executed at least once and that another task continues until a desired state is achieved.

Loop Control Commands

Loop control commands offer refined control over loops, allowing scripts to be both flexible and efficient. The primary loop control commands are Break and Continue and are explained as below:

Break Command

Purpose

The Break command, as its name suggests, is used to break out of a loop entirely, regardless of the loop's condition.

Scenario

Assume you're iterating through a list of files, and you wish to stop the loop entirely once a specific file is found. Instead of waiting for the loop to finish its iterations, the Break command will end the loop immediately upon encountering the specified file.

Continue Command

Purpose

Unlike Break, which exits the loop, the Continue command skips the current iteration and proceeds to the next one.

Scenario

Suppose you're processing items in a queue. If an item meets a certain condition, you might not want to process it but instead move on to the next item. Continue allows this behavior, skipping the current item and advancing to the next.

Sample Program: Working of Loop Control

We shall go back to our system monitoring script and see how these loop control instructions work:

```
$shutdownDetected = $false


Do
{
    # Capture primary system status
    $systemStatus = Get-SystemStatus # Hypothetical cmdlet to get system status

    if($systemStatus -eq 'maintenance_mode')
```

```
    {
        Write-Warning "System is under maintenance. Skipping this cycle."
        Continue
    }

    if($systemStatus -eq 'shutdown')
    {
        $shutdownDetected = $true
        Break
    }


    $connectionAttempts = 0
    $connectionEstablished = $false

    Do
    {
        $connectionStatus = Connect-SecondarySystem # Hypothetical cmdlet to establish a connection
        $connectionAttempts++

        if($connectionStatus -eq 'connected')
        {
            $connectionEstablished = $true
        }
        else
        {
            Write-Warning "Connection attempt $connectionAttempts failed."

            if($connectionAttempts -ge 5)
```

```
        {
            Write-Error "Failed to establish connection after 5 attempts."
            Break
        }

        Start-Sleep -Seconds 5 # Wait for 5 seconds before retrying
    }
}
While (-not $connectionEstablished)


if($connectionEstablished)
{
    # Perform tasks with the secondary system
    Execute-Tasks # Hypothetical cmdlet
}


# Primary system monitoring sleep interval
Start-Sleep -Seconds 60

}
While (-not $shutdownDetected)
```

The script now checks for a 'maintenance_mode' status using the outer loop. If this status is detected, the script issues a warning and skips to the next iteration of the loop using the Continue command. This means the rest of the code in the loop will not execute for that cycle.

In the inner loop, we've incorporated the Break command. After five unsuccessful connection attempts, the script will break out of the inner loop and not continue trying to connect.

Considerations
- Using loop control commands like Break and Continue can greatly improve the efficiency of your script by avoiding unnecessary processing.

- It's important to understand the flow of your loops when using these commands, especially in nested loop scenarios. For instance, a Break command inside a nested loop will only break out of that specific inner loop and not the outer loop.
- Always have a clear logic in mind when employing these loop control commands. Misuse can lead to confusing behaviors or infinite loops.
- Loop control commands are not just reserved for traditional looping structures. They can also be used effectively with other iterative commands like ForEach-Object in PowerShell.

Loop control commands dictate the loop's flow. They provide a means for responding to certain conditions by quitting the loop or skipping a loop iteration. Understanding and executing these commands correctly will help streamline your scripts, making them faster and more responsive to changing situations.

Summary

A thorough examination of PowerShell loops, including While loops, Do-While, and Do-Until, was covered in this chapter. Loops, as we've learned, are fundamental programming constructs that enable the repeated execution of blocks of code based on a condition or a series of circumstances. The While loop in PowerShell is notable for its simplicity and utility, with the essential idea being: as long as the condition is true, continue performing the loop.

We then moved on to learning about the Do-While and Do-Until loops, which are variations on the while loop. While they follow similar ideas, their execution differs in the order of testing the condition and running the loop body. The Do-While loop ensures that at least one execution of the loop body occurs before verifying the condition, allowing tasks within the loop to run even if the original condition is not met. The Do-Until loop, on the other hand, runs until a certain condition is met, effectively acting as the inverse of the While loop.

Understanding failures within loops was a key component of this chapter. Loops, while strong, can become a source of failure if not handled properly. It is critical to recognize potential problems and execute appropriate mistake management solutions. We learned approaches for addressing and resolving mistakes that may occur within loop constructions, highlighting the significance of robust and resilient scripting.

Finally, the notion of loop control instructions (particularly Break and Continue) was explained. These instructions provide developers more control over loops, allowing them to dynamically define loop behavior in response to changing situations. Whether it's exiting a loop prematurely or skipping an iteration, these instructions add flexibility and efficiency to loop operation. The integration of these commands was demonstrated through practical examples, highlighting their potential to refine and optimize script behaviors.

Chapter 9: Managing Windows Systems

Windows Management Overview

An integral part of Windows is the Windows Management Instrumentation (WMI) structure. It provides administrators with a consistent framework for both local and remote system management, allowing them to collect data and make changes to a wide range of parameters and components. At its core, WMI provides a standardized architecture for reading and writing data about system configuration, performance indicators, active processes, and much more.

Given the complexities of today's IT infrastructures, as well as the requirement for scalability and automation, PowerShell has emerged as the preferred tool for administering Windows systems. Its integration with WMI increases its power, revealing capabilities that make it indispensable to Windows administrators.

Why PowerShell for Windows Management?

PowerShell isn't just another command-line tool. Its object-oriented nature, paired with the flexibility of .NET, allows for granular control over system components. Instead of dealing with plain text, users handle objects, which can be filtered, modified, and passed across different cmdlets seamlessly.

With the Get-WmiObject cmdlet, for instance, admins can fetch detailed information from the WMI repository. Whether it's understanding system BIOS details, fetching installed software, or monitoring disk health, a single line in PowerShell can achieve what would traditionally require multiple steps or third-party utilities.

A Unified Ecosystem

The WMI system, with its Common Information Model (CIM) classes, provides a structured and consistent way to interface with hardware and software components. PowerShell taps into this vast repository, offering cmdlets tailored for WMI operations. The synergy between WMI's structured data model and PowerShell's object-manipulation capabilities means that intricate tasks become streamlined. Routine tasks, such as system inventory checks, become automated scripts that run with a single command.

Scalability, Flexibility and Extensibility

Keeping track of just one system isn't cutting it in the modern IT world. Companies often have thousands of machines. PowerShell's remote management features, along with WMI's ability to communicate with remote systems, offer a powerful option to manage thousands of machines. Using sessions, administrators can run scripts on remote machines, making large-scale operations more efficient and consistent.

PowerShell allows you to create custom modules, which demonstrates its adaptability. Administrators can create tools that are adapted to the demands of their specific environment. With the WMI system's support, these tools can be as thorough and exact as needed, tapping into the vast amounts of data provided by WMI.

PowerShell's progress is not stagnant. The growth of the Windows operating system and the introduction of tools such as Windows PowerShell Desired State Configuration (DSC) have expanded the scope of system administration. DSC, for example, allows administrators to specify a system's desired state, and PowerShell guarantees that the system maintains this state, showing its proactive management capabilities.

The relationship between PowerShell and the Windows Management Instrumentation system is a model of efficiency, power, and adaptability. Understanding and leveraging this relationship is not only helpful, but also vital for individuals who want to grasp Windows system management.

User Account Management in WMI

User Account Management is an essential aspect of maintaining a secure and efficient computing environment. Efficient account management can reduce security risks and streamline operational activities. For PowerShell developers and administrators, managing user accounts via Windows Management Instrumentation (WMI) provides robust capabilities, making account management activities more manageable and more programmable.

Windows Management Instrumentation (WMI) is a core Windows management technology that allows for system and network administration. It facilitates management tasks like auditing, configuration, and system status monitoring. One of its vital functionalities is user account management. By leveraging WMI, administrators can execute tasks like creating, deleting, or modifying user accounts, both local and domain.

WMI's Role in User Account Management

The primary WMI class for managing local user accounts on a Windows machine is Win32_UserAccount. This class provides information about user accounts defined on a system.

Some of the properties that can be accessed through this class include:

- Name: Represents the account name.

- FullName: Displays the full name of the user.

- AccountType: Indicates the type, such as local or domain account.

- Disabled: Shows if the account is disabled.

- PasswordRequired: Indicates if the account requires a password.

For domain accounts, the interaction is a bit more complex, often involving interfacing with Active Directory services, but WMI provides the foundation to start the process.

Leveraging PowerShell for WMI-based Account Management

Given below is how PowerShell developers can utilize WMI for user account management:

- Fetching User Details: Using the Get-WmiObject cmdlet, developers can retrieve information about user accounts.

Get-WmiObject -Class Win32_UserAccount

This command fetches all the user accounts on the local system, presenting properties like name, domain, and account type.

- Filtering Specific Users: If one wants details of a particular user, the query can be filtered.

Get-WmiObject -Class Win32_UserAccount -Filter "Name='username'"

This command retrieves details of the user with the username 'username'.

- Creating a New User: Although WMI doesn't natively support user creation, it does facilitate user modification. PowerShell developers typically utilize the .NET classes or other cmdlets, like New-LocalUser, to achieve user creation. Still, WMI's strength is in querying and modifying existing user properties.

- Modifying User Properties: For changing user properties, such as disabling an account or changing a password, developers leverage the methods provided by the Win32_UserAccount class.

While WMI and PowerShell together provide robust user management capabilities, there are aspects to consider:

- Performance: Running extensive WMI queries, especially on large domains, can be resource-intensive. It's essential to optimize scripts for performance.

- Security: Ensure that scripts and the environment are secure. Avoid hardcoding sensitive information like passwords in scripts.

- Compatibility: Ensure that scripts are tested across different Windows versions and environments, as there can be variations in WMI classes and properties.

Developers working with PowerShell will find the combination of WMI and PowerShell to be an attractive set of tools for managing user accounts. It represents the current approach to IT: programmable, scalable, and efficient.

File and Directory Management in WMI

Fundamental to every system administrator job is the ability to manage files and directories. Whether it's monitoring storage, processing files, or managing directories, efficient handling is critical to a system's health and performance. Developers and administrators can accomplish these tasks more effectively by combining Windows Management Instrumentation (WMI) and PowerShell.

WMI includes various classes for file and directory management. The namespaces CIM DataFile and Win32 Directory contain the most notable ones.

- CIM_DataFile: Represents any data file on a computer system running Windows. It contains methods and properties related to the file, such as its name, path, size, and more.

- Win32_Directory: Represents a logical directory on a computer system running Windows. This class has properties related to directories, like name, path, and status.

These above classes provide extensive information about files and directories but also allow for actions like renaming, copying, and deleting, albeit with some limitations compared to native PowerShell cmdlets.

File and Directory Operations via WMI

PowerShell developers can access file and directory data with the Get-WmiObject cmdlet. For instance, to fetch details about a specific file:

Get-WmiObject -Query "SELECT * FROM CIM_DataFile WHERE Name='C:\\path\\to\\file.txt'"

For directories:

```
Get-WmiObject -Class Win32_Directory -Filter "Name='C:\\path\\to\\directory'"
```

WMI allows for some basic operations on files and directories:

- Rename: You can rename a file or directory using the Rename method.

```
$file = Get-WmiObject -Query "SELECT * FROM CIM_DataFile WHERE Name='C:\\path\\to\\file.txt'"
$file.Rename('C:\\path\\to\\newname.txt')
```

- Delete: Deleting is straightforward with the Delete method.

```
$directory = Get-WmiObject -Class Win32_Directory -Filter "Name='C:\\path\\to\\directory'"
$directory.Delete()
```

However, tasks like file copy or moving directories are not directly feasible through WMI classes. For such operations, developers would lean more towards PowerShell's native cmdlets.

Registry Operations in WMI

Windows' configuration settings and options are stored in the Windows Registry, a hierarchical database. For system administrators and developers, the registry is a key region that requires frequent inquiries, modifications, and deletions. Windows Management Instrumentation provides classes for interacting with the Windows Registry, particularly within the StdRegProv namespace. This supplier provides instructions for reading and writing to the register.

Accessing Registry Data with WMI

Before diving into the methods, it's worth noting that the registry has several primary hives, each represented in WMI with a numerical constant:

HKEY_CLASSES_ROOT (HKCR) – 0x80000000

HKEY_CURRENT_USER (HKCU) – 0x80000001

HKEY_LOCAL_MACHINE (HKLM) – 0x80000002

HKEY_USERS – 0x80000003

HKEY_CURRENT_CONFIG – 0x80000005

Using these constants, developers can target specific hives during their operations.

To read from the registry, one might use:

$registry = Get-WmiObject -List "StdRegProv"
$key = "SOFTWARE\\Path\\To\\Key"
$registry.GetStringValue(0x80000002, $key, "ValueName")

This would retrieve the string value from the specified location within the HKEY_LOCAL_MACHINE hive.

Writing and Modifying Registry Data

To modify or add new data, the StdRegProv namespace provides several methods based on the datatype:

SetStringValue

SetBinaryValue

SetDWORDValue

SetQWORDValue

SetMultiStringValue

SetExpandStringValue

For instance, to set a string value:

$registry.SetStringvalue(0x80000002, $key, "ValueName", "NewValue")

Deleting Registry Keys and Values

The deletion of registry keys and values is a high-stakes operation, demanding precision. It's achieved through:

- DeleteKey: To remove an entire registry key.
- DeleteValue: To delete a specific value within a key.

Example to delete a value:

$registry.DeleteValue(0x80000002, $key, "ValueName")

And to delete a key:

$registry.DeleteKey(0x80000002, $key)

Enumerating Registry Keys and Values

Enumerating, or listing, is beneficial when developers need an overview of keys or values within a specific path. Methods aiding this include:

- EnumKey: List subkeys within a specified path.
- EnumValues: Enumerate values within a particular key.

Registry Operations Best Practices

- Backup Before Modification: The registry is critical to the functioning of a Windows system. Always back up the registry or the specific keys you're working with before making changes.

- Avoid Hardcoded Paths: Where possible, use variables or dynamic methods to determine registry paths, especially when writing scripts for different environments.

- Understand Permissions: Not all users or scripts have the privilege to read or write to all parts of the registry. Ensure the executing user or process has the necessary permissions.

- Limit Scope of Changes: Only modify or delete the minimal number of keys/values necessary for the task. Broad changes can inadvertently affect system performance or functionality.

- Test in a Controlled Environment: Before deploying any registry change script on a production environment, test it in a sandbox or controlled environment to ensure no unforeseen consequences arise.

Service Management in WMI

System administrators and developers must handle Windows services as part of their daily duties. Windows services are applications that operate in the background and are critical to the correct operation of a Windows system. Windows Management Instrumentation (WMI), when combined with PowerShell, provides a dynamic platform for managing these services, from asking their status to changing their configurations.

Role in Service Management

Everything that goes into managing the services that are part of an OS is a part of service management. This comprises initiating, terminating, configuring, and monitoring services. In a Windows context, these services might range from critical system tasks such as the Windows Update service to third-party applications.

WMI provides classes for developers to communicate with Windows services. Win32_Service is a primary WMI class for service administration. This class represents a service on the Windows operating system and provides methods and properties that make service management easier.

Accessing Service Information

To retrieve details about a specific service using WMI, you can query the Win32_Service class. For example:

```
Get-WmiObject -Class Win32_Service -Filter "Name='wuauserv'"
```

This command fetches details about the Windows Update service (wuauserv). It provides information like the service's display name, current status, start mode, and more.

Controlling Services: Start, Stop, Pause, and Resume

With the Win32_Service class, developers can also control the operation of services:

Start a Service

```
(Get-WmiObject -Class Win32_Service -Filter "Name='wuauserv'").StartService()
```
Stop a Service:

```
(Get-WmiObject -Class Win32_Service -Filter "Name='wuauserv'").StopService()
```

Pause a Service

(Get-WmiObject -Class Win32_Service -Filter "Name='wuauserv'").PauseService()

Resume a Service

(Get-WmiObject -Class Win32_Service -Filter "Name='wuauserv'").ResumeService()

Each of these commands, when executed, sends a control command to the specified service, affecting its operational state.

Modifying Service Configuration

Beyond mere control, developers might need to modify service attributes, such as its start mode (automatic, manual, or disabled). The Change method of the Win32_Service class facilitates this:

$service = Get-WmiObject -Class Win32_Service -Filter "Name='wuauserv'"
$service.Change($null, $null, $null, $null, "Automatic")

In the above snippet, the start mode of the Windows Update service is changed to "Automatic". The $null parameters indicate that other attributes (like display name or path) are left unchanged.

Monitoring Services

WMI's eventing capability allows developers to monitor changes in services. For instance, you can watch for a service's state transition:

Register-WmiEvent -Query "SELECT * FROM __InstanceModificationEvent WITHIN 10 WHERE TargetInstance ISA 'Win32_Service' AND TargetInstance.Name='wuauserv' AND PreviousInstance.State != TargetInstance.State" -Action {
    Write-Host "The Windows Update service state has changed!"
}

This command sets up a listener for the state change of the wuauserv service and notifies the user when it occurs.

Service Management Best Practices

- Understand Service Dependencies: Some services depend on others to function correctly. Before stopping or modifying a service, ensure that no other services rely on it.

- Limit User Interaction: When scripting service changes, minimize the need for user input or interaction. This reduces the possibility of errors and promotes automation.

- Implement Logging: Track changes to services, especially in production environments. Logging provides a record of actions, aiding in troubleshooting or auditing.

- Test in a Safe Environment: Before applying changes to live or critical systems, test your scripts in a controlled setting. This step ensures that the desired outcomes are achieved without unintended side-effects.

PowerShell also offers native cmdlets like Get-Service, Start-Service, Stop-Service, and Set-Service that are more intuitive for some tasks. The choice between WMI and native cmdlets depends on the specific requirements and the developer's familiarity with each approach.

Event Logs and Diagnostics in WMI

Event logs are essential components of Windows operating systems, serving as storage locations for a wide range of system and application messages, from informative notices to serious system problems. These logs are critical for administrators and developers to debug, audit, and understand system behavior. The combination of WMI with PowerShell provides developers with powerful tools for not only accessing, but also manipulating and reacting to these logs dynamically.

Windows event logs record several system actions and states. They are organized into logs such as Application, System, and Security, with each log including events of a similar sort. Every recorded event is identified by its Event ID, source, type, and message.

Tapping into Event Logs

The primary WMI class for accessing event logs is Win32_NTLogEvent. This class represents an event in an event log. By querying this class, developers can retrieve details about specific events.

For example, to fetch the latest ten error events from the System log:

```
Get-WmiObject -Class Win32_NTLogEvent -Filter "Logfile='System' AND EventType=1" -MaxEvents 10
```

The EventType '1' corresponds to error events.

Windows Query Language (WQL) provides a SQL-like syntax that can be employed with WMI to create more advanced queries. This becomes especially handy when filtering or categorizing event log data.

For instance, to retrieve all error events from the past 24 hours:

```
$yesterday = (Get-Date).AddDays(-1)
$query = @"
SELECT * FROM Win32_NTLogEvent
WHERE Logfile='System'
AND EventType=1
AND TimeGenerated >= '$yesterday'
"@

Get-WmiObject -Query $query
```

Retrieving Event Log Metadata

Developers might sometimes need more meta details about the event logs themselves, rather than the individual events. The Win32_NTEventLogFile class comes into play here.

To obtain the size of the System event log:

```
(Get-WmiObject -Class Win32_NTEventLogFile -Filter "LogFileName='System'").FileSize
```

Reacting to Events with WMI Eventing

Dynamic eventing capabilities are also available in WMI, in addition to querying static data. This means you can configure "listeners" to detect and respond to certain system changes, such as new event log entries.

For example, to monitor and respond to any new error event in the System log:

```
$query = @"
SELECT * FROM __InstanceCreationEvent WITHIN 10
WHERE TargetInstance ISA 'Win32_NTLogEvent'
AND TargetInstance.Logfile='System'
AND TargetInstance.EventType=1
"@

Register-WmiEvent -Query $query -Action {
    Write-Host "A new error event has been recorded in the System log!"
}
```

The __InstanceCreationEvent class in WMI helps detect new instances of a given class, here used to identify new events.

Clearing Event Logs

While most logs in Windows have size limits after which they overwrite old events, occasionally, one might need to manually clear a log. Given below is how you do it with WMI:

```
$log = Get-WmiObject -Class Win32_NTEventLogFile -Filter "LogFileName='System'"
$log.ClearEventLog()
```

Beyond event logs, WMI provides classes for various diagnostics purposes. For instance, Win32_DiagnosticSetting and Win32_DiagnosticResult give insights into the system's diagnostic configuration and results, respectively. This can aid developers in assessing system health or understanding performance metrics.

Centralized Event Log Management

The ability to centrally manage event logs becomes critical in large-scale infrastructures running several Windows workstations. WMI's extendable nature shines through here. PowerShell developers can use the -ComputerName argument in WMI operations to remotely retrieve event logs from multiple machines on the network. This provides a consolidated view of logs, allowing for more efficient analysis and troubleshooting.

For instance, to fetch the last five events from the System log of a remote computer named

"Server01":

```
Get-WmiObject -Class Win32_NTLogEvent -ComputerName Server01 -Filter "Logfile='System'" | Select-Object -First 5
```

Event Forwarding is another advanced functionality given by the Windows Event Log Service. This enables specific events from numerous computers (known as event sources) to be routed to a central computer (known as the event collector). While event forwarding is usually configured through the Windows Event Collector service and subscriptions, WMI can be used to manage and query the setups.

Custom Event Triggers

Custom events can be created using PowerShell and Windows Management Instrumentation. This is quite useful for monitoring certain activities or states. For example, if a specific type of problem occurs, you can configure a custom event to send an alert or run a specific script.

```
$query = @"
SELECT * FROM Win32_NTLogEvent
WHERE Logfile='Application'
AND EventCode='1001'
"@

$action = {
    # Custom actions, such as sending an email alert or logging additional details
}

Register-WmiEvent -Query $query -Action $action
```

Performance Implications and Optimization

Event log queries, especially on logs with a vast number of entries, can be resource-intensive. When working with WMI for event log operations, it's crucial to optimize queries:

- Selective Filters: Always use filters to narrow down the event log data you're interested in.

- Batch Processing: If you're processing a large number of events, consider breaking your queries into smaller batches.

- Scheduled Tasks: For regular event log checks, consider using scheduled tasks, so the checks run during off-peak hours, minimizing impact on system performance.

Given that event logs can contain sensitive information, especially the Security log, it's imperative to understand the security implications:

- Access Control: Ensure that only authorized personnel can access and query event logs. Both WMI and the Event Log service have their respective security settings to restrict access.

- Audit Trails: Keep an audit trail of who accessed the logs and when. This can be crucial for compliance and security reviews.

- Encryption: When transmitting log data, especially to remote locations, ensure the data is encrypted. This protects against potential eavesdropping or data interception.

System Updates and Patches in WMI

The IT ecosystem's ongoing and dynamic nature needs the frequent distribution of updates and patches to ensure software security, stability, and performance. For Windows users, this is of paramount importance. A Windows system is always evolving, from small patches that fix minor flaws to major system updates that improve functionality. WMI (Windows Management Instrumentation) is a critical technology for PowerShell developers to manage these updates in a seamless and efficient manner.

In order to facilitate both local and remote access to system component information, Windows Management Instrumentation (WMI) creates a consistent interface for OS, device, user configuration, and other related data. It includes a wide range of system-related actions and data, including those relevant to system upgrades and patches.

Win32_QuickFixEngineering Class

At the core of patch and hotfix management through WMI is the Win32_QuickFixEngineering class. This class provides information about the patches and hotfixes applied to a particular system.

For instance, to retrieve a list of all the patches installed on a system, a PowerShell developer would use:

Get-WmiObject -Class Win32_QuickFixEngineering

This command will return details like the patch description, installation date, and more.

Sorting and Filtering Updates

Given that systems might have a plethora of patches installed, it becomes necessary to sort or filter them for efficient management. For instance, if you need to fetch patches installed in the last 30 days:

$OneMonthAgo = (Get-Date).AddDays(-30)

Get-WmiObject -Class Win32_QuickFixEngineering | Where-Object {$_.InstalledOn -as [datetime] -ge $OneMonthAgo}

Remote Patch Management

Suppose you're managing a network of computers and need to check patches on a remote machine. Using the -ComputerName parameter, developers can retrieve such details without physically accessing the remote system.

Get-WmiObject -Class Win32_QuickFixEngineering -ComputerName "RemotePC01"

While managing updates, it's essential to understand the types of patches:

- Security Updates: Address vulnerabilities that might be exploited by malicious entities.

- Critical Updates: Correct issues affecting crucial software components but aren't security-related.

- Service Packs: A collection of updates, fixes, and enhancements delivered in one package.

Windows Server Update Services (WSUS) allows IT administrators to manage the distribution of Microsoft product updates released through Microsoft Update. With PowerShell and WMI, developers can automate many WSUS-related tasks. By targeting the Microsoft.Update namespace, they can fetch details about pending updates, install them, or even decline them.

Windows Firewall Management

Windows Management Instrumentation (WMI) has emerged as a centralized tool for managing numerous Windows features, including the firewall. Windows Firewall is an integrated software firewall and packet filtering solution. When it comes to protecting networks, both internal and external, it is the first line of protection. It operates by establishing a set of rules that determine which traffic is permitted or prohibited depending on port, protocol, and source/destination address.

Navigating NetFirewall Namespace

WMI's root\StandardCimv2 namespace provides the classes necessary for Windows Firewall management. Within this namespace, various classes like MSFT_NetFirewallRule offer granular control over firewall rules and configurations.

One of the first tasks a PowerShell developer might execute is listing the existing firewall rules:

```
Get-CimInstance -Namespace root\StandardCimv2 -ClassName MSFT_NetFirewallRule
```

This command retrieves all the firewall rules configured on the system, providing a comprehensive view of the system's current traffic management stance.

For more specific insights, such as determining active inbound block rules, a PowerShell developer might use:

```
Get-CimInstance -Namespace root\StandardCimv2 -ClassName MSFT_NetFirewallRule | Where-Object { $_.Direction -eq 'Inbound' -and $_.Action -eq 'Block' -and $_.Enabled -eq 'True' }
```

Creating new rules is fundamental in customizing and enhancing the security posture. To add an inbound rule that allows traffic on port 8080, one would use:

```
$ruleProps = @{
    DisplayName  = 'Custom_Inbound_8080'
    Direction    = 'Inbound'
    Action       = 'Allow'
```

```
    Protocol    = 'TCP'
    LocalPort   = '8080'
    Enabled     = 'True'
}
```

New-CimInstance -Namespace root\StandardCimv2 -ClassName MSFT_NetFirewallRule @ruleProps

Over time, firewall rules may require adjustments. Using WMI and PowerShell, developers can modify rules seamlessly. For instance, to change the action of a rule:

$rule = Get-CimInstance -Namespace root\StandardCimv2 -ClassName MSFT_NetFirewallRule -Filter "DisplayName='Custom_Inbound_8080'"

$rule.Action = 'Block'

Set-CimInstance -InputObject $rule

As security needs evolve, certain rules may become obsolete. They can be easily removed:

Get-CimInstance -Namespace root\StandardCimv2 -ClassName MSFT_NetFirewallRule -Filter "DisplayName='Custom_Inbound_8080'" | Remove-CimInstance

Windows Firewall operates under different profiles: Domain, Private, and Public. Each profile can be in an "On" or "Off" state. Managing these profiles is integral:

Check the state of the profiles
Get-NetFirewallProfile

Set a profile's state
Set-NetFirewallProfile -Name 'Public' -Enabled False

With Windows Management Instrumentation (WMI) and Windows Firewall so closely linked, they form a formidable duo for PowerShell developers. It enables the detailed administration of traffic regulations, ensuring that systems are protected from potential risks while preserving critical connectivity.

Group Policy Management in WMI

One of Windows' most essential features, Group Policy lets admins set and enforce settings on Active Directory objects, including users and computers. PowerShell developers benefit from the ability to administer and interact with Group Policy via Windows Management Instrumentation (WMI), which opens up new opportunities for automation and configuration.

Group Policy enables centralized management of settings in a Windows system. System settings, software deployment, security setups, and user environment customisation are all under the purview of these policies, which can be applied to either systems or users.

WMI provides a collection of interfaces via which PowerShell can communicate with various system components, including Group Policy. For Group Policy, the root\RSOP (Resultant Set of Policy) namespace in WMI becomes particularly relevant.

Accessing RSOP Data

RSOP data gives a cumulative view of all the policies that apply to a user or computer. Using PowerShell with WMI, developers can query this information:

```
Get-CimInstance -Namespace root\RSOP\Computer -ClassName RSOP_SecuritySettingNumeric
```

This command fetches the RSOP data for numeric security settings applied to the computer.

Filtering GPOs for Specific Settings

Often, it's necessary to find which Group Policy Object (GPO) is responsible for a particular setting:

```
Get-CimInstance -Namespace root\RSOP\Computer -ClassName RSOP_GPO | Where-Object { $_.Name -eq 'SpecificGPOName' }
```

Retrieving GPO Details

Understanding the specifics of a GPO, such as its GUID or when it was last applied, is crucial:

```
Get-CimInstance -Namespace root\RSOP\Computer -ClassName RSOP_GPO
```

The application of a GPO is determined by its link to an Active Directory site, domain, or organizational unit. PowerShell developers can manage these links:

```
# List GPO Links
Get-GPInheritance -Target 'OU=Sales,DC=Contoso,DC=com'

# Block GPO Inheritance
Set-GPInheritance -Target 'OU=Sales,DC=Contoso,DC=com' -IsBlocked $true
```

Modifying Group Policy Settings

While WMI can be used to read RSOP data, direct GPO modification is typically achieved through PowerShell cmdlets rather than WMI:

```
# Create a new GPO
New-GPO -Name 'CustomGPO'

# Configure a setting in the GPO
Set-GPRegistryValue -Name 'CustomGPO' -Key 'HKEY_LOCAL_MACHINE\Software\Custom' -ValueName 'Setting' -Type String -Value 'Value'
```

Backup, Import, and Restore Operations

Regular backups of GPOs ensure that they can be restored in case of misconfigurations:

```
# Backup a GPO
Backup-GPO -Name 'CustomGPO' -Path 'C:\GPOBackups'

# Restore a GPO
Restore-GPO -Name 'CustomGPO' -Path 'C:\GPOBackups' -BackupId 'BackupGUID'
```

Security Filtering and Delegation

PowerShell allows developers to manage who a GPO applies to and who can edit/manage the GPO:

```
# Add a security filter
Set-GPPermission -Name 'CustomGPO' -TargetName 'Domain Users' -TargetType Group -PermissionLevel GpoApply

# Set delegation
Set-GPPermission -Name 'CustomGPO' -TargetName 'Domain Admins' -TargetType Group -PermissionLevel GpoEditDeleteModifySecurity
```

Summary

We began our in-depth investigation of the Windows Management Instrumentation (WMI) system and its connection with PowerShell in this chapter, highlighting its unparalleled capabilities for Windows systems management. WMI is a fundamental aspect of Windows and provides interfaces and tools for managing numerous Windows components, configurations, and systems. Its capabilities include from user accounts, file systems, registry activities, and even complex administration features such as Group Policies.

We delved deeper and discovered how user account management in WMI gives you power over establishing, changing, and deleting user accounts. This functionality is crucial for large enterprises and IT departments seeking seamless user management operations. Furthermore, as we looked into file and directory management, we learned how WMI may provide information and control over files, directories, and associated characteristics. This, when combined with PowerShell's extensive scripting capabilities, can result in automated and efficient file system management. Similarly, PowerShell's registry operations via WMI enable reading, writing, and editing the Windows registry, allowing for in-depth system changes and configurations.

The subtleties of service administration, event logs, and diagnostics emerged, emphasizing WMI's importance to system administrators and developers. Service administration in WMI with PowerShell allows you to initiate, stop, and alter Windows services. At the same time, event logs and diagnostics provide information about the system's health, operations, and potential faults. These features, when combined, ensure that developers and administrators may proactively fix issues, resulting in smooth system operations.

In addition, system updates, patches, and firewall management revealed the extent of WMI's functionality. Using WMI with PowerShell, developers can query, update statuses, apply patches, and guarantee that systems are up to date and safe. Rules, configurations, and policies on the firewall can all be changed to ensure maximum system protection.

Finally, we looked into Group Policy management using WMI. Group Policies, which are a foundation of Windows systems for centralized configuration management, may be intricately maintained with WMI and PowerShell. This chapter provided you with a thorough grasp of the integration and capabilities of WMI, PowerShell, and Group Policy Management. It covered fundamental operations like creating and linking GPOs as well as complex functionality like security filtering and ASGM.

Chapter 10: Remote Systems Management

Remote Management with PowerShell

System administrators and information technology professionals frequently find that remote system management capabilities are more of a need than an advantage. PowerShell's "remoting" capability really changes the game when it comes to remote management. It's incredibly versatile and full of genius. This chapter provides an overview of PowerShell's remote management features, covering topics such as remote commands, secure communication channels, session management, debugging remote connections, and recommended practices.

Remote Commands and Management

The linchpin of PowerShell's remote management is the capability to execute commands on a remote computer. This is achieved through cmdlets like Invoke-Command, which allows one to run scripts or commands on distant systems seamlessly. This capability eliminates the need to physically access a machine or use third-party remote software.

Secure Communication Channel

As we propel into an era where security breaches and cyber threats are rampant, ensuring secure communications, especially in remote operations, is paramount. PowerShell remoting leverages the WS-Management protocol, which operates over the standard HTTPS port, ensuring encrypted and secure communications. This means that all communications between the local and remote machine are encrypted, safeguarding data and commands from prying eyes.

Session Management

PowerShell offers what is known as "sessions" for remote management. A session, in this context, refers to a persistent environment on the remote machine where commands can be executed. There are two main types of sessions: one-time sessions which are temporary and are discarded after execution, and persistent sessions, often referred to as "PSSessions", which can be reused. Managing these sessions efficiently ensures a consistent environment for executing remote commands.

Troubleshooting Remote Connections

Even with a tool as robust as PowerShell, encountering issues during remote connections is not uncommon. These can range from authentication errors, network issues, or configuration discrepancies. The capability to identify and rectify these issues is an invaluable skill. This chapter sheds light on common problems and their resolutions, ensuring uninterrupted remote operations.

Best Practices for PowerShell Remoting

Tapping into the vast potential of PowerShell remoting also comes with the responsibility to use it judiciously. There are best practices that professionals should adhere to. For instance, always using secure channels, limiting remote access only to required systems, setting appropriate permissions, and routinely auditing remote sessions. These practices ensure not just effective but also safe utilization of PowerShell's remote capabilities.

As we progress further into this chapter, we will dissect each of these areas in-depth, furnishing you with both the knowledge and the tools to harness the full prowess of PowerShell's remote management.

Enabling Remote Management

The first and most important step in taking advantage of PowerShell's remote management capabilities is getting your environment ready to receive and handle remote connections. This is necessary since PowerShell remoting is disabled by default for Windows clients. However, on most Windows Server editions, it is. Now we shall take a closer look at how to allow remote management in the Windows environment.

Pre-requisites

- Windows Version Compatibility: Ensure you're operating on Windows 7 or later for client systems and Windows Server 2008 R2 or later for server environments.

- PowerShell Version: Ensure you have at least PowerShell v2.0, though having the latest version is always recommended for added functionality and security.

Setting up Environment

PowerShell remoting is based on the Windows Remote Management (WinRM) service, which uses the WS-Management protocol. The initial step is to ensure the WinRM service is set to auto-start and is currently running.

You can use the following commands to achieve this:

```
Set-Service WinRM -StartMode Automatic
Start-Service WinRM
```

PowerShell's execution policy determines how (or if) PowerShell loads configuration files and runs scripts. For remoting, it's advisable to set this policy to RemoteSigned. This ensures scripts can run, and only scripts that are from the internet and not locally created require a signature from a trusted publisher.

To set this policy, use:

Set-ExecutionPolicy RemoteSigned

Enabling Remoting

This is achieved with a simple cmdlet:

Enable-PSRemoting -Force

The -Force parameter ensures that you aren't bombarded with confirmations at every step. This cmdlet performs several actions:

It runs the Set-WSManQuickConfig command, which performs several tasks:

- Starts the WinRM service.

- Sets the startup type on the WinRM service to Automatic.

- Creates a listener to accept requests on any IP address.

- Enables a firewall exception for WS-Management traffic.

Adjusting Firewall

PowerShell remoting requires certain ports to be open on the firewall. The Enable-PSRemoting cmdlet typically manages this for you, but it's always wise to double-check and understand these settings. By default, it uses port 5985 for HTTP and port 5986 for HTTPS.

If you need to manually configure the firewall, you can use the following:

New-NetFirewallRule -Name PSRemoting -Protocol TCP -LocalPort 5985 -Action Allow

Verifying Configuration

Once the initial setup is complete, always ensure that the configuration is correct. Use the Test-WsMan cmdlet to ascertain this. If the configuration is correct, this command will return system information of the computer you specify:

Test-WsMan -ComputerName <YourComputerName>

Configuring Remoting and SSL

By default, only members of the Administrators group on a computer can establish remote sessions to it. If you need to allow non-admin users to create sessions, you'd have to modify the session configurations. This is an advanced topic, but in a nutshell, you'd use the Set-PSSessionConfiguration cmdlet.

For enhanced security, especially when dealing with crucial systems, consider using SSL to encrypt your remote sessions. This requires an SSL certificate but offers a significant security boost over standard connections.

Configuring Trusted Hosts

Sometimes, you might need to connect to computers that aren't in the same domain or lack certificates. In such cases, you'd rely on the TrustedHosts configuration. This isn't a recommended practice for production environments due to security implications, but it's useful for testing or trusted intranet scenarios.

To configure TrustedHosts:

```
Set-Item wsman:\localhost\client\trustedhosts -Value *
```

The * value allows connections from any computer, but in a real-world scenario, you'd specify hostnames or IPs.

The true challenges arise when diving into sessions, invoking commands, and maintaining security. As we proceed, we will explore each of these areas, ensuring you're well-equipped to manage systems remotely, efficiently, and securely.

Secure Communication Channels

Security must be prioritized when overseeing systems from a distance. The same is true for PowerShell remoting. The entire basis of remotely managing machines—whether executing commands, accessing data, or configuring systems—requires that the communicated data remain secure and tamper-proof. This is when encrypted communication routes come into play.

Need for Secure Communication Channels

Data in its unprocessed state is vulnerable to interception, manipulation, and even imitation by bad actors. This becomes even more important when the data contains system configurations, administrative commands, or sensitive information. Hence, the difficulty is to ensure:

- Confidentiality: Ensuring that the data being communicated between machines remains private.

- Integrity: Ensuring that the data is not altered in transit.

- Authenticity: Ensuring that the communication is happening between the intended machines.

PowerShell remoting leverages the WS-Management protocol, which provides support for both HTTP and HTTPS. While HTTP is adequate for scenarios within a trusted network, HTTPS brings the much-needed SSL/TLS layer to guarantee the three principles mentioned above.

Setting up Secure Communications
SSL/TLS with PowerShell Remoting
Using SSL/TLS is the most recommended way to secure PowerShell remoting. It provides encryption, ensuring data confidentiality and integrity. Below is how to set it up:

- Obtaining an SSL Certificate: You'd need a valid SSL certificate from a Certificate Authority (CA). This could be a public CA for wide-scale operations or a private CA for internal purposes.

- Configuring the WinRM Listener: Once you have the certificate, configure the WinRM service to use this certificate for its HTTPS listener. Use the following command:

New-Item -Path WSMan:\LocalHost\Listener -Transport HTTPS -Address * -CertificateThumbprint <Your-Cert-Thumbprint> -Force

Replace <Your-Cert-Thumbprint> with the thumbprint of your SSL certificate.

- Connecting Using HTTPS: When initiating a remote session, ensure that you specify HTTPS as the protocol. For instance:

Enter-PSSession -ComputerName RemoteServer -UseSSL

SSH as a Transport
With the evolution of PowerShell, especially with the introduction of PowerShell Core (cross-platform), SSH (Secure Shell) has been added as a transport option. SSH is a protocol that provides a secure channel over an unsecured network.

To use SSH for PowerShell remoting:

- Ensure both source and target machines have SSH server and client components installed and configured.

- To initiate a session, use:

Enter-PSSession -HostName <RemoteServer> -UserName <UserName> -SSHTransport

Securely Storing and Using Credentials

While not directly a communication channel, the method by which credentials are handled during remote sessions is a significant security consideration.

- Prompting for Credentials: The Get-Credential cmdlet prompts the user to input their credentials securely:

$myCred = Get-Credential

Enter-PSSession -ComputerName RemoteServer -Credential $myCred

- Using Windows Credential Manager: For scripts or automated processes, consider integrating with the Windows Credential Manager, ensuring credentials aren't hardcoded or exposed.

Kerberos for Domain Scenarios

For environments that are part of a domain, Kerberos authentication becomes the default and is a secure method for authenticating users. As long as the machines are part of the same domain or trusted domains, Kerberos ensures mutual authentication between client and server without sending passwords.

Just Enough Administration (JEA)

JEA is a security feature in PowerShell that allows precise delegation of administration tasks. It enables you to define what users can do, on which systems, and under what conditions. It limits the exposure to administrative credentials and reduces the risks associated with privilege escalation.

Configuring Trusted Hosts

For non-domain scenarios where HTTPS/SSL isn't viable, there is the TrustedHosts list. This list, as previously learned, can be set to trust certain hosts. Though less secure, it's an option when you're sure about the trustworthiness of the network.

While these methodologies bolster the security of PowerShell remoting, it's crucial to approach them in line with the organization's security policies and requirements.

Managing Sessions in PowerShell

Session management is an essential aspect of PowerShell remoting. It deals with establishing, utilizing, and terminating the communication between a client and a remote machine. Proper session management ensures optimal resource utilization and a smooth remoting experience.

What is a PSSession?

A PSSession is essentially a user environment where PowerShell commands are run. It's an instance of PowerShell on a local or remote machine. While you can use remoting for one-off commands without manually managing a session, there are benefits to creating and managing sessions explicitly.

Creating a New Session

The primary cmdlet for this task is New-PSSession. Given below is how you can establish a session:

```
$session = New-PSSession -ComputerName "RemoteServerName"
```

This command establishes a session with the specified remote server. The session is stored in the $session variable for further management and utilization.

Using an Established Session

Once a session is created, you can use it for executing commands or scripts. This ensures that the same environment is used, which can be beneficial if there are specific configurations or variables set in that session.

To invoke a command on a session:

```
Invoke-Command -Session $session -ScriptBlock {
    Get-Process
}
```

This runs the Get-Process command on the remote server using the established session.

Managing Multiple Sessions

PowerShell allows you to manage multiple sessions simultaneously. This is particularly useful for performing tasks across a range of servers or endpoints.

$sessions = New-PSSession -ComputerName Server01, Server02, Server03

This establishes sessions to three different servers.

To run a command across all these sessions:

Invoke-Command -Session $sessions -ScriptBlock { Get-EventLog System }

This retrieves the System event log from all three servers.

Reusing Sessions

One of the major benefits of PSSessions is the ability to reuse them. Without explicit session management, each remoting command would create a new session, use it, and then discard it. This overhead can be significant when running many commands. By reusing sessions, you sidestep this overhead.

For instance, if you've set a particular variable or loaded a specific module in a session, you don't have to redo that for every command.

Disconnecting and Reconnecting Sessions

You might not always want to maintain a live connection. PowerShell allows you to disconnect from a session and then reconnect later. This is beneficial for long-running tasks or if you need to free up local resources temporarily.

To disconnect:

Disconnect-PSSession -Session $session

To reconnect:

```
Connect-PSSession -Session $session
```

You can view all the active sessions:

```
Get-PSSession
```

This will list all sessions, their IDs, and their states (e.g., Opened, Disconnected).

Removing Sessions

When done with a session, it's good practice to remove it, freeing up resources on both the client and server sides.

```
Remove-PSSession -Session $session
```

Setting Session Configuration

PSSessions use configurations, which are essentially a set of rules or policies for the session. You can set the amount of memory a session uses, which cmdlets are available, etc. These configurations ensure sessions have the resources they need and operate securely.

To retrieve available session configurations:

```
Get-PSSessionConfiguration
```

In essence, session management in PowerShell remoting is about establishing a balance between performance and convenience.

File Transfer to Remote Systems

One typical task in system administration and automation is transferring files to remote systems. When PowerShell is used, this operation becomes more efficient, allowing administrators to send and receive data over remote sessions. Within this framework, we will explore the inner workings, techniques, and factors to be considered when transferring files using PowerShell.

Why Transfer Files?

Before diving into the techniques, we shall understand the requirement:

- Configuration & Automation: Deploy configuration files, scripts, or software packages across servers.

- Data Collection: Fetch logs, data dumps, or other files from remote systems for analysis.

- Patch & Update Deployment: Distribute patches, updates, or new versions of software.

Cmdlets and Techniques for File Transfer

PowerShell doesn't offer a direct cmdlet like "Send-File" or "Receive-File". Instead, it integrates file transfer capability within its broader remoting and session features.

Using Copy-Item with PSSessions

One of the most straightforward methods to transfer files is by using the Copy-Item cmdlet in conjunction with PSSessions. This leverages the established remoting infrastructure for file operations.

Example: Sending a File to a Remote Machine

```
$session = New-PSSession -ComputerName "RemoteServerName"
Copy-Item -Path "C:\localpath\myfile.txt" -Destination "C:\remotepath\" -ToSession $session
```

The above commands establish a PSSession with a remote server and then utilize the Copy-Item cmdlet to transfer "myfile.txt" from the local machine to the remote server.

Example: Fetching a File from a Remote Machine

```
$session = New-PSSession -ComputerName "RemoteServerName"
Copy-Item -Path "C:\remotepath\myfile.txt" -Destination "C:\localpath\" -FromSession $session
```

Here, the roles are reversed, fetching "myfile.txt" from the remote server to the local machine.

PowerShell and SMB

Server Message Block (SMB) is a network file sharing protocol that allows applications to read and write to files and request services. While not exclusive to PowerShell, SMB can be used alongside it for file operations.

Example: Using SMB with PowerShell

```
New-PSDrive -Name X -PSProvider FileSystem -Root
"\\RemoteServerName\sharedfolder"
Copy-Item -Path "C:\localpath\myfile.txt" -Destination "X:\"
```

This creates a temporary mapped drive using SMB and then copies the file to the remote share. While this method is straightforward, ensure the required permissions are set on the shared folder.

Using BITS (Background Intelligent Transfer Service)

BITS is a Windows component that provides asynchronous file transfers. It's advantageous when transferring large files as it can resume interrupted transfers and uses bandwidth efficiently.

The primary cmdlet to work with BITS is Start-BitsTransfer.

Example: Transferring File with BITS

```
Start-BitsTransfer -Source "C:\localpath\myfile.txt" -Destination "\\RemoteServerName\remotepath\"
```

This initiates an asynchronous file transfer. To monitor its progress, you can utilize the Get-BitsTransfer cmdlet.

PowerShell offers a range of options for transferring files to remote systems. Whether you're using direct cmdlets like Copy-Item with PSSessions, leveraging network protocols like SMB, or opting for advanced services like BITS, it's about choosing the right tool for the job.

PowerShell Remoting Best Practices

In addition to ensuring that your operations are effective, implementing best practices guarantees that they are also safe and in compliance with regulations.

Use Encrypted Channels

Situation

Imagine a large organization with several departments. The HR department, dealing with sensitive employee data, uses PowerShell remoting to fetch certain data from multiple servers. If this data is transferred over unencrypted channels, there is a potential risk of data theft.

Best Practice
Always use encrypted channels like HTTPS or SSH for remoting. With WinRM, configure it to use HTTPS. This ensures that all data transferred between the host and remote is encrypted, reducing the risk of eavesdropping.

Employ JEA

Situation
John, a junior administrator, needs to restart a particular service on all servers. However, giving him full administrative rights might be risky, as a wrong command could lead to disruptions.

Best Practice
Use JEA to give John only the permissions he needs. This principle ensures that users get the minimum required access for their tasks. By setting up a JEA endpoint, John can only restart the specific service without having broader system access.

Regularly Update and Patch

Situation
Sarah, a seasoned admin, has been using PowerShell for years. But she hasn't updated it in a while. A new vulnerability, which attackers could exploit, is discovered in the older version she's using.

Best Practice
Regularly update and patch not just PowerShell but also its dependencies, such as .NET. This ensures that you're safeguarded against known vulnerabilities.

Avoid Hardcoding Credentials

Situation
Mike develops a script for regular backups and includes the admin credentials directly in the script. If an insider threat or a malicious entity gets hold of the script, they'll have high-level access.

Best Practice
Use secure methods like the Windows Credential Manager or employ certificates. If you need to supply credentials in a script, use the Get-Credential cmdlet to prompt the user for them, instead of hardcoding.

Limit Scope of Remoting

Situation
Lucy wants to pull log files from ten specific servers out of a hundred. Instead of broadcasting

her remoting request, she should target only those ten servers.

Best Practice
Always narrow down your remoting scope to the specific machines you intend to work with. Avoid using wildcards that could affect more systems than necessary. This reduces unnecessary load and potential errors.

Validate Inputs and Outputs

Situation
A script developed by Jake fetches data from remote servers and processes it. One day, due to an unexpected input, the script behaves erratically, causing data corruption.

Best Practice
Always validate data going into and coming out of your scripts. This includes data fetched from remote sessions. Ensuring data integrity can prevent unexpected behaviors and potential system crashes or corruption.

Keep Audit Logs

Situation
After a massive system failure, the IT department wants to trace back the commands that led to the disaster. Without logs, pinpointing the root cause becomes a guessing game.

Best Practice
Always log your remote sessions, especially in production environments. Tools like Start-Transcript can be invaluable. Not only does this help in troubleshooting, but it also ensures accountability.

Test in Controlled Environment

Situation
Oliver, eager to deploy his newly written script, pushes it directly to the production servers. An overlooked bug in the script causes a significant system downtime.

Best Practice
Always test your scripts and commands in a controlled environment before deploying them to production. A sandbox or a separate testing environment can help catch issues early.

Avoid Overloading Remote Machines

Situation
Emily has a script that fetches vast amounts of data from remote servers, processing it locally. The remote servers experience a slowdown every time the script runs.

Best Practice
Be mindful of the resources your commands might consume on the remote end. Fetch only the necessary data, or better yet, process data remotely and then retrieve the results, ensuring remote servers aren't unduly burdened.

The path to mastery involves not just knowing the commands, but understanding the implications of each action, being proactive in ensuring security, and having the foresight to predict and prevent potential issues.

Summary

The emphasis of this chapter was on PowerShell remoting, a powerful tool that allows developers and administrators to easily execute commands on remote computers. The foundation was built with a brief overview of remote management, emphasizing the importance of distant tasks in current IT infrastructures. To use this functionality, the initial configuration is critical. We looked at enabling remote management for the existing Windows environment, making sure that the system is configured to send and receive remote commands.

Security remains crucial, particularly when connecting via networks. This chapter emphasized the need of creating secure communication routes in PowerShell. It is not only about ensuring connectivity, but also protecting data flow from any dangers. utilizing encrypted channels such as HTTPS when utilizing WinRM helps to protect data integrity and secrecy. Aside from secure connections, session management was another key topic. PowerShell allows you to create, manage, and terminate sessions, thus understanding the session lifecycle is critical for successful resource management. The ability to send files to remote systems expands the capabilities of PowerShell remoting. Files may be transferred with a few instructions, making operations such as script deployment and log retrieval more efficient.

Finally, no instrument is effective unless it is used in accordance with established criteria. We looked at the best practices that every PowerShell developer should follow. This not only ensures effective operations, but also reduces risk. Practices such as Just Enough Administration (JEA) stress issuing only the essential permissions to avoid potential misuse or accidents. The highlighted practices included regularly updating PowerShell, eliminating hard-coded credentials, limiting the scope of remote access, and maintaining audit logs. Each exercise was reinforced with actual circumstances, demonstrating how they would play out in real-world situations. The chapter prepared you to use PowerShell remoting safely, efficiently, and responsibly.

Thank You

Index

A

Access Control 184
Administration 198, 206
Audit Trail 184
Automation 4, 21, 49, 73, 76, 202

B

Breakpoints 12, 50, 51, 135, 136, 137, 140, 145

C

Code Block 101
Command-Line 23, 24
Configuration 2, 7, 11, 172, 179, 195, 201, 202

D

Debugging 12, 15, 50, 64, 71, 118, 122, 128, 129, 135, 136, 137, 138, 139, 140, 145, 158
Dependencies 70, 72, 154, 180
Deployment 7, 21, 59, 202
Development Environment 13, 73
Directory Management 174
Do-Until 160, 161, 162, 164, 168
Do-While 149, 160, 161, 162, 164, 168

E

Encryption 184
Error Handling 53, 74, 80, 154
Event Logs 180, 182

F

File Transfer 201, 202
Firewall 195

G

Group Policy 188, 189, 191

I

Interface 11, 45

L

Log Management 182

P

Patches 184
Policy Management 191

R

Registry Operations 175, 177
Remote Session 4, 13, 137, 138
Remote Systems 192, 201
Remoting 193, 195, 196, 197, 203, 204

S

Secure Communication 193, 196, 197
Service Management 178, 180
Session 30, 56, 138, 139, 140, 193, 199, 200, 201
Session Management 56, 193
Stack Traces 142, 143
System Monitoring 30, 122, 152, 161
System Update 184

T

Troubleshooting 1, 5, 121, 193, 210

U

User Account 172

W

While Loops 146, 147, 152, 154, 158
Windows Firewall 186, 187
Windows System 170
WMI32, 112, 171, 172, 173, 174, 175, 178, 179, 180, 181, 182, 183, 184, 185, 186, 187, 188, 189, 190, 191
Workflow 5

Epilogue

Upon completion of this illuminating journey through the PowerShell cosmos, you, my esteemed reader, will emerge changed. You've gone deep, swam in the convoluted seas of automation, ascended the difficult peaks of scripting, and emerged with a thorough grasp over this amazing technology. "PowerShell Troubleshooting Guide" served as a mentor as well as a guide, lighting the road, challenging conventional ideas, and demanding nothing less than excellence. You stepped up to the plate, fearlessly tackling every obstacle, becoming an expert in every detail, and finally cementing your spot among the elite group of PowerShell enthusiasts.

You've come a long way from knowing the fundamentals to decoding the complexities of remote network administration, from building simple yet effective scripts to diagnosing the most complex of problems. It's a testament not only to PowerShell's potency, but also to your unwavering focus, commitment, and passion for the trade.

However, like with any knowledge, the actual test is application. The world outside of this book is full with obstacles, unusual events, and changing landscapes. The Windows ecosystem is dynamic, with increasing demands for system administration and automation. However, with your arsenal of abilities and insights, you're more than prepared to negotiate this terrain. Remember that each problem is an opportunity to use what you've learned, to innovate, and to constantly improve your approach. Accept these obstacles because they will shape your path from educated practitioner to recognized expert.

It is critical to remember that the field of technology is always evolving. New tools evolve, ideas shift, and what is deemed cutting-edge today may be obsolete tomorrow. But that is precisely where PowerShell shines. Its underpinnings, logic, and essence remain unwavering in the face of change. And with the foundation you've gained from this book, you'll be able to investigate, adapt, and master any new advances that come your way.

While this book may have come to an end, your adventure with PowerShell is just getting started. There is a world out there bursting with opportunity, ready for you to write new success stories, automate previously perceived complicated procedures, and conjure solutions that have a lasting impact. The tales, examples, and real-world scenarios you encountered were more than simply lessons; they inspired you to think outside the box, challenge the existing quo, and promote the cause of efficient, effective, and exceptional automation.

Finally, let this not be a farewell, but a new beginning. Allow your newfound knowledge to be the wind beneath your wings, propelling you to greater heights. Allow the problems you face to serve as a crucible for testing and honing your skills. And may your experience with PowerShell serve as a reminder of the endless possibilities that await those who dare to dream, study, and succeed.

Remember, as you end this book, that you're not only armed with commands, scripts, and functions. You bring a legacy, a tradition of excellence, and a dedication to continuous growth with you. Here's to a voyage full of discoveries, innovations, and successes. May you always be a lighthouse for people in the world of PowerShell and beyond. Have a safe journey, my reader, and may your code always be true.

Made in the USA
Monee, IL
03 May 2026

49438433R00129